# CHICKEN ON THE GRILL

### RECIPES FOR CHICKEN, DUCK, PHEASANT, TURKEY AND OTHER BIRDS

BY
DAVID BARICH AND THOMAS INGALLS

PHOTOGRAPHY BY
DENNIS BETTENCOURT

FOOD STYLING BY
ROBERT BURNS

 HarperPerennial

*A Division of* HarperCollins*Publishers*

*We would like to thank the following stores
and individuals who helped make this book
look the way it does.*

Cottonwood, Fillamento, Darlene Carlson,
Clervi Marble, Gumps, Dandelion/Tampopo,
Panetti's Gifts, Vero, Zonal, Mosaic Gallery,
Virginia Breier, Paul Lagatutta/John Whitehall,
Nicholas Petras, Bell'occhio, Marlene Sanchez,
Susan Kohlik, Marcia Stuermer, Galisteo,
Forrest Jones, Hedy & Shug Matsuno, Angie
Chan, Sally Schmidt, Barbara Takiguchi,
Susan Eslick, The Gardener, Cedanna, Sylvan
Marshall, Rudi and Susan Legname, Barb,
Produce Manager, Real Food Co. 24th Street,
Summer House Gallery.

For information address
HarperCollins Publishers Inc.
10 East 53rd Street
New York, NY 10022

Printed in Japan.

FIRST EDITION

Book and Cover Design:
Ingalls + Associates
Designers: Tom Ingalls and Tracy Dean
Photography: Dennis Bettencourt
Photographer's Assistant: Jean Lannen
Food Stylist: Robert Burns
Prop Stylist: Alison Anthony
Studio Assistance: Willie Walker

**Library of Congress Cataloging-
in-Publication Data**

Barich, David

    Chicken on the grill
          p.          cm.
    Includes bibliographical references and
indexes.
    ISBN 0-06-096890-7 (pbk.) : $17.00
    1. Barbecue cookery.   2. Cookery
(Chicken)   I. Ingalls, Thomas.   II. Title.
TX840.B3B35   1992
641.5'784--dc20
                                91-58480
                                CIP

92 93 94 10 9 8 7 6 5 4 3 2 1

This creature, almost alone, is our chief resource when friends or guests arrive suddenly and unexpectedly; we owe to the chicken all the splendor displayed by a rich table or by one that is modestly supplied or by that which is slenderly laden. If there is need for an elegant and groaning board, you have in the chicken the most praiseworthy meat.

—*Aldrovanni on Chickens: The Ornithology of Ulisse Aldrovanni*

# CONTENTS

# INTRODUCTION

In the world of food, not many things are as comforting or as enticing as a plump bird cooked over glowing coals. Surely this was one of our earliest foods, as grilled birds in almost endless variations are now found in cuisines around the world. Partly because of this archetypal memory, perhaps, grilled chicken is a dish that almost everyone loves, so it's always a good choice for entertaining. When you consider also the low-fat and low-calorie content of chicken, turkey, and most other birds, you will understand why we decided to devote an entire book to the subject of grilled birds.

Chicken, along with turkey, *poussin,* squab, quail, and Cornish hen, has another delightful quality: The mild-tasting meat of these birds can be complemented by most flavors, so that the choice of marinades, sauces, and other flavoring agents is almost infinite. The richer-tasting flesh of pheasant, partridge, duck, and goose lends itself to assertive flavors such as those of rosemary, ham and bacon, aromatic woods, and intense sauces. Most of the recipes in this book are for chicken, but we have also included recipes for turkey, Cornish hen, *poussin,* quail, squab, pheasant, and duck. Part of the fun of grilling, of course, is experimenting, so if you want to use a particular marinade or sauce on a different bird than the one specified in the recipe, please do.

These recipes were developed and tested using naturally raised free-range chickens, a superior food that is worth seeking out for reasons of taste as well as health. We believe that naturally raised chickens have a better taste and texture than do factory-raised birds, and that their flesh is more tender. But this type of chicken is not essential to the creation of a successful dish—a standard supermarket chicken can be grilled to perfection if you follow a few simple guidelines.

*Chicken on the Grill* contains twenty-five recipes for chicken and other birds. Each recipe headnote includes suggestions for accompanying dishes and beverages (see the List of Recipes, page 89, for a list of recipe titles plus suggested accompaniments). Often, at least one of the companion dishes will be grilled also, to make double use of the coals, while a second will be a dish to prepare in the kitchen before or during grilling. We have included several recipes for sauces made from a reduction of the marinade; this can be done quickly while the bird rests under its aluminum foil cover (covering the bird for several minutes after grilling is a technique that helps retain the juices and ensures that the meat will be moist when served).

In general, our recipes were planned to serve 4 to 6 people, but any of them can be increased to serve a larger group. Because cold grilled foods have a more intense charcoal-smoke flavor, we like to cook extra to have leftovers for sandwiches and salads.

In the last decade, grilling has become the quintessential cooking technique in this country. It has a long history here, from the planked and smoked fish of the Northwest Indians and the cowboy campfires to the country pit barbecues, family campfires, and fifties patio parties. Grilling partakes of the ancient mystique of cooking in the open air, with all the rustic appeal of the fragrance of charcoal and wood smoke.

The new flavors and foods that have become available to us in the last decade are now found in stores all across the United States and have changed our way of cooking. The accessibility of these diverse ingredients, combined with a freedom and willingness to combine different ingredients in completely new ways, has made grilling more interesting and rewarding.

Our recipes were inspired by a variety of places and eras, from the classic barbecue sauce of Kansas City to some of the innovative flavor combinations of new American cuisine. Many dishes reflect the growing influence of Asian ingredients, such as hot chili paste and fish sauce, in American cooking, but others use such classic European ingredients as balsamic vinegar and sweet basil.

It's the combination of primitive and sophisticated, down-home and exotic that has made grilling so popular today. The recipes in this book were created to explore all of these possibilities, and to help you get even more pleasure from cooking on the grill.

CHAPTER 1
# A GUIDE TO THE GRILL

# A Guide to the Grill

Poultry and game birds are excellent for grilling, as their relatively fatty skin acts as a natural insulating and basting element for the flesh. The challenge in grilling birds is to make sure that the skin is crisp while the interior remains moist. Grilling is an inexact art compared to most cooking methods; this is part of its appeal. But the advances in grill technology over the last decade have taken a lot of the guesswork and most of the awkwardness out of outdoor cooking, while leaving the incomparable flavor of grilled food.

Here are some of the most commonly available grills, plus our favorite tools and grill accessories.

## Grills

**The Kettle Grill:** The most ubiquitous of American grills, this shiny metal cooker with its rounded removable cover has many good qualities. Sturdily built, affordable, and relatively easy to keep clean, it can be used as an open grill for searing or quick cooking, or covered with its lid for the longer cooking of larger pieces of food, including whole turkeys. Because it is light in weight, it gets taken to picnics, and its two wheels allow it to be rolled easily from place to place. The fancier kettle grills have tool holders, fold-away lids, and built-in thermometers.

The major disadvantage of the kettle grill is that the height of the cooking rack is not adjustable, so that the distance between the food and the coals is fixed. This limitation can be counterbalanced by the use of the cover; by adjusting the vents in the cover and in the base of the grill (the bottom vent is also the outlet for ashes that accumulate in the fuel grate); and by careful monitoring of the degree of the fire's heat, which can be altered by simply moving the coals closer together for more heat and farther apart for less.

**The Kamado:** This distinctive-looking ceramic cooker is made in Japan and is available in several different sizes and colors. Although it is more expensive and much heavier than a kettle grill, it is definitely the next step up for the grilling enthusiast, and it's an excellent choice for large pieces of food such as roasts and whole chickens and turkeys, and any other food that needs long, slow cooking. The kamado cooks more slowly than kettle or console grills do, so cooking times for these grills will need to be altered accordingly.

Although the cooking rack is fixed some distance from the coals, the thick walls and the shape of the kamado enable it to function as a grill oven, much like the *tandoor* of India. It has a removable interior ceramic ring that radiates heat evenly throughout the cooker, giving it the capabilities of a convection oven. The kamado can also be used as a smoke oven: An optional removable top piece has adjustable vents with which to regulate the amount of smoke inside the kamado.

Because of its insulating construction, the kamado needs relatively little fuel. It gets hotter than other kinds of grills do (up to 500°) and stays hotter longer, so it works best for the long cooking of large pieces of food and can even be used to bake bread. The kamado rests in a wheeled metal basket, and so is relatively mobile.

**Console Grills:** Outdoor grills have become more and more elaborate, and some now are the size of a kitchen stove. These rectangular grills use either charcoal or gas tanks and can be wheeled from place to place. The cooking rack is usually banked by work surfaces, some with inset cutting boards, so the problem of where to put food, dishes, and utensils is solved. A variety of attachments, an interior thermometer, a hood, and sometimes even a second rack unit make cooking on these grills almost as convenient as cooking on a traditional range in your own kitchen.

**Gas Grills:** Although they have their detractors, gas grills are here to stay—literally, in some cases, because those using natural gas must be installed with a stationary gas line. They are expensive compared to most other grills, but they take much less time and effort to prepare for cooking. Grills using LP gas tanks are movable, and both movable and stationary gas grills will give you the flavor of smoke from the cooking food, a result of the juices burning on the lava rocks that line the fuel bed.

The fragrance of charcoal will be missing, however, although the manufacturer of one model of portable gas grills advertises that the special metal bars under its cooking rack do add a charcoal flavor to foods.

Some gas grills have individually controlled burners that can be set to precise cooking temperatures. All gas grills have hoods, and most of them have rotisserie attachments, so they are great for roasting chickens for large groups of people.

**Other Covered and Uncovered Grills:** A wide variety of other kinds of grills exists, from the hibachi to the brick backyard barbecue to the built-in kitchen or fireplace grill. The primary distinction among these grills is whether or not they have a cover. Uncovered grills are best for the fast grilling of small pieces of food, and thus their repertoire is limited to such things as hamburgers, some vegetables, and kabobs. You can approximate a cover with a wok lid or a

tent of aluminum foil, but for serious grilling you should avail yourself of a grill with a removable tight-fitting cover.

**Charcoal-Water Smokers:** These tall, cylindrical smokers concentrate the smoke from charcoal and smoking woods in their narrow confines. Built in layers, beginning with a fuel grate and a water pan topped by one or more cooking racks, they have adjustable vents to control the level of smoke. People who love smoked foods swear by these grills, which produce moist foods strongly flavored with wood smoke. Any of the recipes in this book that use smoking woods can be adapted to a charcoal-water smoker by following the manufacturer's instructions.

## CHARCOAL AND WOOD

**Mesquite Charcoal:** The trend toward mesquite cookery is based on mesquite's excellence as a fuel. This lump charcoal burns faster and hotter than do other fuels, and it lends its particular mild fragrance to grilled foods. When you first light it, mesquite will send off an alarming amount of sparks, so it's important to stand away from the fire and make sure that your grill is not near any flammable materials. You can break up any large pieces of mesquite with a hammer, but remember that it catches fire and burns quickly, so don't make the pieces too small. Unburned lumps of mesquite can be relighted and used a second time.

Because mesquite burns at such a high temperature—up to 1,000°—the initial stages of a red-hot fire may be too hot for searing or fast grilling. When grilling poultry or game birds, take care not to put them on the fire at its hottest stage, as they will burn quickly (see "Know Your Fire," page 16).

The one disadvantage of mesquite and other hardwood charcoals is that they can be hard to find in many parts of the country. If you are dedicated to good grilling, the solution is to order enough mesquite and/or other hardwood charcoal by telephone or mail to last you through the year. Thanks to 800 numbers and credit cards, this is simple; see Mail-Order Sources on page 86 for the addresses and telephone numbers of hardwood charcoal suppliers.

**Hardwood Charcoal:** Other woods besides mesquite, such as oak and ash, are made into lump charcoal. Like mesquite, they burn cleanly, with a minimum of ash. They also burn hotter than do briquettes, but at their hottest they burn at around 800°—not quite as hot as mesquite. Also like mesquite, they add their particular subtle fragrance to food, and leftover lumps can be relighted and used again.

**Wood:** Wood takes longer to reach the grilling stage of coal-readiness (about 1 hour), and it has a higher ash content than does lump charcoal. Using half hardwood charcoal and half wood is a good way to add the fragrance of wood smoke to your dish. Make sure that the wood you use is whole, untreated hardwood, not softwood or any kind of processed wood, including lumber, that might contain chemicals.

**Briquettes:** Try to avoid cooking with briquettes if at all possible. Although they are cheaper in purchase price, they add chemical off-tastes to your food and polluting gases to our air. Because they are made with fillers and binders, they have a higher ash content than do lump charcoals, so you will need to use more briquettes for any given grilling session. Briquettes also burn cooler than lump charcoal does, around 600°, so they are not as effective for searing and open grilling.

## Preparing the Fire

**Laying the Charcoal:** For hardwood charcoal, spread a layer of large chunks over an area slightly larger than the area the food will cover on the cooking rack. For briquettes, spread a layer 2 briquettes deep. If the recipe calls for more than 20 minutes of grilling, start with a larger quantity of charcoal to allow for the longer cooking time.

**Lighting the Charcoal:** Try not to use liquid charcoal starter. Not only does it impart its chemical taste to food, it is damaging to the environment. And it's really not necessary—electric starters, kindling, or charcoal chimneys are just as fast, and all of these methods are safer, as well.

The simplest method of lighting charcoal is to use hardwood **kindling** with a wad or two of newspaper under it. Place charcoal over the kindling, open the bottom

vents of the grill, and light the newspaper (leaving some air space between the briquettes and the kindling).

If you have an electric outlet near your grill, an **electric starter** may be your best choice, although it does take slightly longer to get a charcoal fire started. Place the starter under the coals and then plug it in. Remove the starter as soon as the first coals are lighted—this usually takes 10 minutes or so.

What started out as a large coffee can with holes punched in the sides (with a beer opener) for ventilation is now sold as a tall black metal cylinder with a handle, and is the most popular alternative to liquid starter. Because the **charcoal chimney** confines the charcoal in a smaller air space, kindling is not needed; instead, 1 or 2 sheets of crumpled newspaper are placed in the bottom section of the chimney, and medium-sized chunks of lump charcoal are piled in the top. The cooking rack is removed, the bottom grill vents are opened, and the chimney is placed on the fuel grate. Now the newspaper is lighted, and the chimney sits until the top layer of coals are lighted but not flaming. At this point, the lighted coals are dumped onto the fuel grate.

This inexpensive device will eventually pay for itself because of the money you will save by not purchasing liquid starter. Its also simpler, cleaner, and safer to use, and it's just as reliable.

Now available in natural foods stores and some super-markets, **wax fire starters** have no additives. They are excellent for camping and picnics, when you might not want to bring along the charcoal chimney.

## Preparing the Cooking Rack

Make sure the cooking rack is clean every time you cook. The best way to do this is to clean the rack with a wire grill brush immediately after each use—it's much easier to clean the rack when it's warm and food hasn't had too much of a chance to cook onto the metal.

If the cooking rack has been kept clean it's not usually necessary to oil the rack before cooking, unless you are grilling delicate fish or food that has a fragile coating. If you didn't clean the rack after your last grilled meal, you may have to use steel wool; in this case, oil the grill before cooking again in order to season the metal.

After the coals have been lighted, put the cooking rack in place over the coals so that the rack will be hot when food is placed on it—this will help the food to cook evenly.

## KNOW YOUR FIRE

The key to good grilling is knowing your fire. A slew of variables, including the temperature of the air and the amount of wind, can affect a fire's heat level and the rate at which the fire burns. Learning to gauge the heat of the fire lets you know when to start grilling and when to adjust the heat level for fast- or slow-burning fires, and consequently how to adjust cooking times. It's all a matter of attention to detail, plus a little experience.

Plan on allowing 45 minutes to elapse from the time you light the charcoal until you are ready to grill; hardwood requires about 1 hour. There are three distinct stages of heat for a charcoal or wood fire:

**Red Hot:** At this level, glowing red coals will be covered lightly with white ashes. If you hold your hand about 6 inches from the cooking rack at this stage, you will have to move it away after 3 or 4 seconds. This is the stage for searing and for quick grilling. Be sure not to put food on the grill if the fire is any hotter than this.

**Medium-Hot:** When the fire is medium-hot, you will barely be able to see the red glow of the coals through a thicker layer of ashes, and you will be able to keep your hand 6 inches from the rack for 5 to 7 seconds. This is the best stage for covered grilling.

**Low:** At this stage, the coals are completely gray, with no visible red glow. A low fire is best for long, slow cooking of foods in a covered grill.

## REGULATING THE FIRE

If the fire is burning too slowly or too fast for your purposes, three simple methods will allow you to regulate the heat:

**1. Adjusting the Vents:** Open the bottom and top vents of the grill to let more air into the grill and make the fire burn hotter. Partially close the vents to cool down the fire. (The bottom vent of a kettle grill also serves as an outlet for ashes from the bottom of the fuel grate.)

**2. Adjusting the Coals:** Move the coals apart or away from the food on the cooking rack to lower the heat of the fire, or move the coals closer together to intensify the heat. Arrange the coals into a circle around the food, or to one side of the grill, to allow the food to cook by indirect heat when the grill is covered; in this case, you may want to put a metal drip pan under the food.

**3. Knocking Off the Ashes:** If the coals have built up a thick layer of ashes and you want the fire to burn a little hotter, simply shake the grill or tap the coals with a grill utensil to remove the ashes.

If the fire is ready and you're not, put the cover on the grill with the vents partially closed; this will slow the fire until you're ready to grill.

## COVERED GRILLING

Most of our recipes specify searing or browning the bird over red-hot or medium-hot coals on an open grill, then covering the bird to finish cooking. Open grilling without a cover is best reserved for quick-cooking foods such as sausages, hamburgers, and sliced vegetables. Covering the grill lowers the heat of the fire and helps ensure a juicy grilled bird. Unless you are cooking a whole bird or adding smoking woods or other flavor-enhancers to the coals, keep the upper vents on the grill cover open. You can also cover the grill and partially close the upper vents if you are trying to lower the heat of the fire before adding food to the cooking rack (see "Regulating the Fire," above).

## INDIRECT GRILLING

"Indirect grilling" simply means that the food is not directly over the coals as it cooks in a covered grill. This technique makes your grill, in essence, a grill roaster, and should be be used for large pieces of food, such as roasts and whole chickens, that need a longer time to cook. For higher and more even indirect heat, move the burning coals into a circle, place a drip pan in the center, and place the food to be grilled over the drip pan (use this method for a whole turkey). For slightly lower indirect heat, move the coals to one side of the fuel grate, place a drip pan on the other side, and place the food over the drip pan. You will need to turn the food occasionally to cook it evenly. A third method, which is the one we use most often in this book, is the simplest of all:

Just move the bird to one side of the grill with one side facing the coals; turn it 180 degrees to the other side once or twice during the grilling process to cook and brown it evenly. We usually don't bother with a drip pan or with moving the coals for food that cooks in less than an hour.

## FLARE-UPS

If you are careful not to use too hot a fire, you will avoid most flare-ups. If flare-ups do occur, move the food to the side of the grill and wait until the fire has burned down. Partially closing the vents and covering the grill also will dampen most flames, as will moving the coals apart. You should keep a spray bottle of water handy to douse any flare-ups that seem to be unmanageable.

## COOKING TIMES AND JUDGING DONENESS

Although we have tested and timed all our recipes, our cooking times must be considered suggestions only, as there are so many variables that affect how fast food cooks on the grill. The temperature of the food, the fire, and the air are important factors, as is the level of humidity and whether or not it's windy outside. On damp days, food will cook more slowly; wind will make the fire burn hotter. As we mentioned earlier, hardwood charcoal, including mesquite, burns hotter than briquettes.

All of our recipes specify that the food should be at room temperature at the time it's put on the grill. This is one of the most important things you can do to ensure good grilling; it gives you more control over the length of cooking time, and will allow any food to cook more evenly.

Experience in grilling and attention to detail will help you learn how to judge the heat of a fire and and when food is perfectly cooked. An instant-read thermometer is the most reliable aid in judging doneness, and an in-grill thermometer will help you maintain the correct level of heat.

Because of the growing incidence of salmonella, it is important that chicken be cooked thoroughly. If the chicken is red at the bone or the flesh is not opaque throughout, it should be cooked longer. Chicken and other birds are considered done and safe to eat when a thermometer inserted into the inside of the thigh, and not touching a bone, registers 180°. All-white meat pieces of poultry are done when a thermometer inserted into the center of the flesh registers 170°. Whole stuffed birds are done when a thermometer inserted into the stuffing registers 165°.

For whole or half chickens, a time-honored test for doneness is that of piercing the skin of the thigh with a knife; if the juices run clear, the chicken should be done. Another sign of doneness is when the leg of the chicken moves easily in its socket. Experienced grillers can judge doneness by appearance alone: If the breast meat has begun to separate horizontally, the skin on the legs has begun to pucker, and the chicken has begun to shrink slightly all over, it is done.

Judging the doneness of smaller pieces of chicken is a little more difficult. In the case of chicken breasts, some people use the "feel" test: When done, the chicken should have the same springy quality when pressed with your index finger as does the fleshy part of the palm at the base of your thumb. When in doubt, we advocate the simplest and most effective test of all: Remove the chicken from the grill to a plate and cut into it with a knife to make sure the flesh is opaque throughout.

**Please note:** Our recipes specify boned whole chicken breasts with skin, as we feel they cook more evenly and stay juicier. If you use boned half breasts, the cooking time will be a little shorter than that specified for whole breasts; if you use breasts with the bone in, you will need to add a few minutes more, as chicken with the bone cooks a little slower.

## REPLENISHING THE COALS

A charcoal fire will burn for about 1 hour before it needs new coals. New mesquite added to a low fire will be ready to cook over in 10 to 20 minutes; briquettes will take a little longer. To save time, light coals in a charcoal chimney set on heatproof surface about 10 minutes or so before you think you will need them; you will be able to proceed with your cooking right after the fully lighted coals are added to the fire.

## Adding Flavors to the Fire

All of our recipes for grilled chicken call for covered cooking after an initial searing or a few minutes of browning on each side; we think this is the best method for cooking juicy, tender chicken. Covered grilling is also a fine opportunity for adding extra flavor to chicken with the use of aromatic woods and herbs. Smoking woods are now available in bits, chips, and chunks. The most common wood types are hickory and mesquite, but you also will find oak, olive wood, apple, and other fruit woods.

Wood bits are usually soaked in water and sprinkled over the coals anytime you want to add a light smoke touch to foods. Follow the directions on the packaging for preparing wood chips; usually these are soaked in water for about 30 minutes. Wood chunks will need to soak for about 1 hour. If you use your own smoking woods, be sure not to use treated lumber. Remember not to overdo on the amount of wood chips or chunks—you don't want their smoky flavors to overpower the delicate taste of most poultry.

Other flavor enhancers for the grill are vine cuttings, fresh or dried herb sprigs and twigs, dried fennel branches, bay leaves and branches, and fresh or dried citrus rinds. Use grapevines for a simple grilled chicken without a strongly flavored marinade; their flavor is subtle. Fresh or dried citrus rinds, like wood chips and chunks, should be soaked in water before being added to the fire; use them to complement birds with a citrus marinade. Fresh or dried herbs should also be soaked and used to complement birds whose marinade, stuffing, or sauce uses the same herb or herbs. Dried fennel branches, the dried leaves and branches of bay trees (also called laurel trees), and fresh or dried sprigs and/or branches of rosemary and thyme are among the best choices of herbal flavorings to add to your coals.

## Storing Charcoal

If you plan to do much grilling at all, we suggest buying several large bags of mesquite or other hardwood charcoal and dumping them all in a large plastic or metal trash can with a tight-fitting lid. Keep the can right next to your grill, where it will stay dry and available for use anytime you get the urge to fire up the coals.

## Cleaning the Grill

As we mentioned earlier, by far the best time to clean the cooking rack is immediately after use. A wire grill brush is indispensable for this task. Cleaning the cooking rack with a wire brush takes hardly any time when the rack is still warm. If you do have to resort to steel wool to clean a cold cooking rack, season it by rubbing cooking oil on the grids.

## Putting the Fire Out

If you have an open grill without a cover, you should pour a little water over the coals and check them later to make sure they have gone out. If you have a covered grill, just close all the vents and cover the grill. If you have used hardwood charcoal, you will usually be able to use the leftover coals the next time you cook: To light used coals, smother them with new lighted coals from the charcoal chimney.

## Tools for the Grill

In the last few years, a number of grilling tools have been developed that help make grilling much easier. Following are the tools that we find either helpful or essential.

**Charcoal Chimney:** Unless you have an electric starter or an always available stash of kindling, you should buy a charcoal chimney. You'll never have to deal with liquid starter again.

**Long-handled Tongs:** These metal tongs are spring loaded, so they have more control. Look for the ones found in restaurant supply stores; they are more strongly built and are reasonably priced. This all-purpose utensil is best for picking up pieces of food; it can also be used to adjust coals, and its scalloped spoon-like tips can be used for basting.

**Wire Grill Brush:** This tool is the answer to the problem of how to keep the cooking rack clean, an essential step in good grilling. A clean cooking rack prevents foods from sticking to the grill, and ensures that rancid or off flavors of cooked foods won't affect your current grilled dish.

**Instant-Read Thermometer:** A little more expensive than regular food thermometers, but worth it. The instant-read thermometer immediately gives you the interior temperature of foods and is most helpful in preventing either the undercooking or overcooking of chicken and other birds.

**Grill Mitts:** These extra-long, heavy-duty mitts are an important accessory for the grill. Even if you don't use oven mitts in your kitchen, you should invest in a grill mitt.

**Spray Bottle:** Keep a spray bottle filled with water on hand as a last resort in putting out flare-ups.

**Bent-Blade Spatulas:** The turning surface of the spatula is at an angle to the handle, which makes this spatula much easier to use and gives you more control when turning food. Choose the long-handled variety made for grilling. You will need one for turning delicate foods such as breaded chicken or fish fillets, and small pieces of foods such as vegetables.

**Basting Brushes:** Although a long-handled brush for basting is not essential (you can use a big spoon or the tip of your tongs), it is nice to have one.

**Skewers:** Soak wooden skewers in water for at least 15 minutes before using to keep them from burning up on the grill. Thread medium-sized pieces of food on 2 parallel wooden or metal skewers to prevent the food from turning.

**Timer:** It's easy to lose track of time, especially when cooking for a group, as is often the case with grilling. Use a kitchen timer and reset it for each phase of the grilling process. Look for the type that clips onto your apron—you'll be sure to hear it ring.

**Grill Thermometer:** Designed to be kept inside a covered grill, this thermometer will give you more control over long-cooked foods such as whole chickens and turkeys.

**Drip Pans:** Metal pie pans make good drip pans and can be easily cleaned and reused if they are soaked right after using.

**Marinade Pans:** For marinating foods, you can use almost anything except uncoated aluminum, which tends to give acidic foods such as tomatoes, vinegar, wine, and citrus juice a metallic off taste. We prefer shallow oval baking dishes of either glass or ceramic for small pieces of poultry and game birds, and large glass or ceramic bowls for whole and halved birds.

**Grill Baskets:** These hinged wire baskets make it easy to turn fish, either whole or in pieces, and are great for grilling vegetables. You don't really need them for poultry and game birds unless you are cooking a large quantity of serving pieces at once.

**Grilling Grids:** Operating on the same principle as the grill basket, these perforated metal sheets with handles sit on top of the cooking rack and are used to grill small pieces of food that would otherwise fall through the grids of the cooking rack. However, the foods must be turned, preferably with a bent-bladed spatula, for grilling on the other side. You don't need one for cooking birds, but it would be a fine addition to your collection of grill accessories.

**Knives:** Good knives are essential to any kind of cooking.

**Cutting Board:** For cutting up raw chicken, it's best to have a plastic or acrylic cutting board that is kept solely for use with flesh foods. These inexpensive cutting boards will not harbor bacteria as do wooden cutting boards. Be sure to wash your cutting board with hot soapy water after each use; plastic or acrylic boards may be washed in a dishwasher.

**Carving Board:** Not necessary, but nice to have. Wooden boards made especially for carving have grooves that will collect the juices of chicken and other birds.

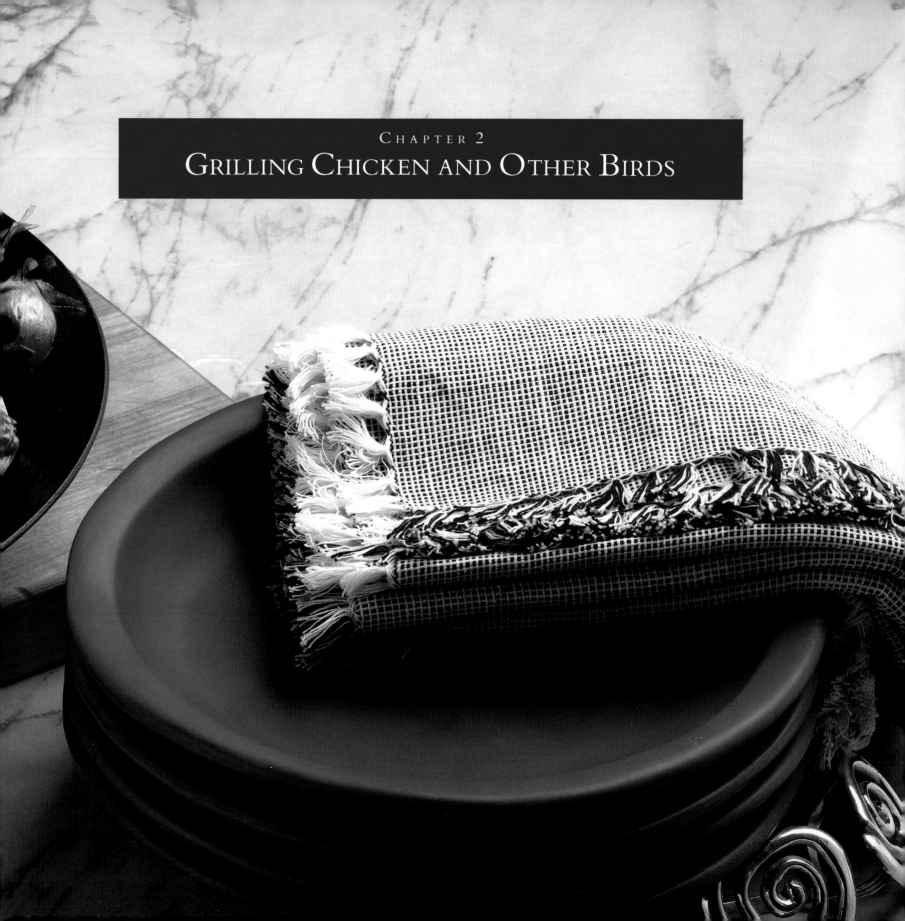

# CHAPTER 2

# GRILLING CHICKEN AND OTHER BIRDS

# GRILLING CHICKEN AND OTHER BIRDS

Although most of our recipes are for chicken, we have included quail, pheasant, turkey, Cornish hen, duck, squab, and *poussin* in this book. Below is a brief glossary of birds and information on cooking them over charcoal or wood.

## A GLOSSARY OF BIRDS FOR THE GRILL

**Capon:** Use a capon as a substitute for pheasant, or any time you want to cook a large, tasty bird that is not quite as large as a turkey. This castrated male chicken usually weighs from 6 to 8 pounds, and is best when cooked whole over a low fire in a covered grill. Its rich meat is complemented by intensely flavored marinades and sauces.

**Chicken:** The most commonly available of all birds, chicken is endlessly adaptable to the grill, as the range of flavors that will complement its mild-tasting flesh is limited only by the chef's ingenuity. Chickens range in size from the *poussin* (see below) to the stewing hen. The various categories of chickens reflect their age. As they mature and grow in size, their flesh becomes less tender and their breastbone calcifies, changing from cartilage to bone. The fryer, broiler, or broiler-fryer (the names are interchangeable) weighs from 2 to 4 pounds and is 7 to 13 weeks old; the roaster, a little older, ranges from 4 to 7 pounds; and the stewing hen, which must be stewed or braised to tenderize its tough flesh, can weigh 8 pounds and may be 10 months old or more.

Although its flesh is relatively low in fat, the skin of the chicken is fatty and should be left on during grilling to act as a natural basting element. We think chicken is best when cooked briefly first on an open grill, then covered to finish cooking and to preserve its juiciness. Whole or half chickens will benefit from covered indirect grilling using a drip pan. Naturally raised free-range chickens that have not been fed artificial stimulants or kept penned in cages have the best flavor and texture, are lower in fat, and are worth their higher price.

**Cornish Hen:** These small (1- to 2-pound) birds are an excellent product with the great advantage of availability: They are sold frozen in most supermarkets and may be substituted for *poussins* and squabs. Their delicate-tasting flesh should be paired with mild marinades and sauces.

**Duck:** Although ducks do not yield as much meat per pound as do most other birds, their meat has an incomparable rich flavor that has become a favorite of leading chefs over the last decade. Domestic Long Island and Pekin ducks are excellent products, available both whole (weighing 4 to 5 pounds each) and cut into breasts, which are great for grilling. The breast of the Muscovy duck is especially large, around 2 pounds, and is the best choice for grilling if you can find it.

Because duck has a relatively high percentage of fat, it is essential to grill it covered, using indirect heat and a drip pan. It is also essential to prick the skin of a whole duck all over before and during grilling. The distinctive flavor of duck is beautifully complemented by the flavors of charcoal and wood smoke, and by a host of assertive fruit, herb, and vegetable flavors. Soaked apple wood chunks or chips are a nice addition to a charcoal fire when grilling duck.

**Goose:** Like duck, goose has a fairly high fat content, and it should be grilled in the same manner: Prick the skin before and during cooking, and grill it covered, over indirect heat, using a drip pan. Also like duck, the assertive flavor of goose meat marries well with the fragrance of grill smoke and intensely flavored marinades and sauces. Geese usually weigh from 6 to 10 pounds and will serve about 1 person per pound.

**Partridge:** These little birds range from just under a pound to about the size of quail. Like pheasant, they are raised on farms in the United States. Their somewhat chewy texture takes well to long marinating, and they are excellent grilled whole. Substitute partridge for quail in most recipes, and match them with the same flavors as suggested for quail, below.

**Pheasant:** Once available only to hunters, pheasant is now being farm raised in several states across the country and is thus increasingly available. Young and adult pheasants range in size from 1 to 2½ pounds and may be substituted for chicken in all grilling recipes. Their taste is similar to that of chicken, though more flavorful, and their meat has more texture. Pheasant is complemented by the flavors of fruit, wines and other spirits, wild rice, and root vegetables.

**Poussin:** These young chickens have long been a favorite in France for their all-white, extremely tender flesh. Sometimes called "squab broilers" because of their small size, *poussins* are around 25 days old. They are now being marketed in specialty meat markets in this country and are worth seeking out, as their juicy meat is a natural for the grill. Ranging in size between 1 and 2 pounds, 1 *poussin* can be substituted for 2 Cornish hens in all grill recipes. *Poussins* are usually best matched with flavors that will not overwhelm their mild taste.

**Quail:** Like pheasant and squab, more and more quail are being farm raised in the United States and are increasingly available to the home cook. Two kinds of quail now on the market are Texas bobwhites, which have white breast meat, and the smaller, all-dark-meat Georgia quail.

Quail are lean, relatively tiny birds usually weighing less than 6 ounces; they should always be marinated before being cooked on a covered grill to keep them from drying out. Try to find boned quail, as they are easier to eat; they will also cook more evenly (the rib cage and backbone are removed, but the wing and leg bones remain). Take care not to overcook these little birds, and make sure your fire is not too hot. Quail go well with foods that have a ripe or woodsy flavor, such as dried fruits, brandy and fruit liqueurs, *pancetta* and prosciutto, and whole grains.

**Squab:** These young pigeons have a dark, juicy flesh that is especially good grilled. Usually weighing under 1 pound, they are farm raised and are available in many specialty meat markets. Squab may be substituted for *poussins* and Cornish hens in all grill recipes. They are good with the same autumnal flavors suggested for quail.

**Turkey:** Grilled whole turkey is a great change from the standard roast Thanksgiving bird, and it's also marvelous for parties and large dinners at any time. Choose naturally raised birds for their superior flavor and tender flesh. Thanks to the turkey marketing industry, this bird now is available in many supermarkets in a variety of other forms, from ground turkey to whole breasts with or without bones, as well as cut into legs, thighs, and breast fillets—all of which can be grilled. The rich flavor of turkey is complemented by the flavor of charcoal and may be enhanced with a variety of smoke flavors, from hickory chips to fresh or dried herbs.

## COOKING CHICKEN AND OTHER BIRDS SAFELY

In the last few years, a rise in the number of outbreaks of salmonella has focused attention on the way in which chickens are processed for the market. The consensus seems to be that the combination of mass production methods and a reduction in the number of federal food inspectors has increased the incidence of salmonella in chickens. Although no statistics exist to prove that hand-processed chickens are less likely to carry this bacteria, you might prefer to buy naturally raised, hand-processed birds not only for their taste and chemical-free meat, but also for the probability that more careful processing will result in a salmonella-free product.

No matter what brand of chickens you buy, however, it is important to follow a new set of guidelines for cooking with chicken and other birds today. Indeed, similar guidelines apply to all flesh foods and any foods of animal origin, including all fish, meats, eggs, and milk.

• Refrigerate uncooked birds as soon as possible after purchasing. Don't leave chicken or any other animal foods in your car or anywhere else for any length of time en route from market to home, especially when the weather is warm. If you know your trip from store to home will take over half an hour, bring along a cooler for storing milk, eggs, and flesh foods.

• Wash your hands with soap and hot water before handling raw birds. Wash the bird inside and out under cool running water; dry with paper towels and discard the towels.

• Use one cutting board, preferably an acrylic or plastic one, for flesh foods only; cut all other foods on a different board.

• After handling or cutting raw birds, wash your hands, utensils, and cutting board well in hot soapy water. Remember to wash sponges, dish towels, and dishcloths, too. Do not handle any other foods without first washing your hands.

• Don't let chicken and other birds marinate at room temperature for more than 2 hours. To be ultra safe, marinate birds under refrigeration.

• Any marinade to be used as a sauce after the bird is cooked should be boiled for several minutes before serving.

• Be sure to wash in hot, soapy water any dish in which an uncooked bird was marinated, and any vessel that was used to transfer the bird to the grill. Take care that any juices from the uncooked bird do not come into contact with other foods.

• Stuff whole birds right before grilling, and test the stuffing with a thermometer before serving the bird; the stuffing should reach a temperature of 165°.

• Cook chickens and all other birds until the meat is no longer pink at the bone, the internal temperature reaches 180° when a thermometer is inserted on the inside of the thigh (make sure it is not touching bone), and the juices run clear when a thigh is pierced with a knife. All-white-meat portions of turkey and chicken should be cooked to 170°; the flesh should be opaque throughout when cut into with a knife.

• Remove all the stuffing from stuffed whole birds to serve. Refrigerate the bird and the stuffing separately.

• All cooked birds should be refrigerated within 2 hours of being cooked.

## PREPARING BIRDS FOR THE GRILL

Follow the cleanliness guidelines above in handling uncooked birds. Remember to wash uncooked birds inside and out under running cool water. Remove all visible fat from birds to be grilled, as the fat will melt and fall onto the hot coals, causing unnecessary smoke and flare-ups.

**Stuffing Whole Birds:** Make sure the bird is rinsed, then patted dry inside and out with paper towels. Lightly salt and pepper the interior of the bird, and fill the bird loosely with stuffing just before grilling. The stuffing will expand and will become more moist than the same stuffing cooked separately in a baking dish.

**Trussing Whole Birds:** You may want to use trussing pins or skewers to close the cavity of a stuffed bird; lacing the trussing string tightly around the pins or skewers keeps the stuffing from falling out or becoming dry. You can also close the opening with fresh herbs or a chunk of apple or onion, depending on the stuffing ingredients.

Trussing is not necessary, but it does keep a bird shaped into a compact, plump bundle that is easier to grill and much more pleasing when served. The classic French trussing method uses a long thick needle threaded with cotton string, but you can prepare a bird for grilling without it. Although this method may be confusing at first, after you've done it a couple of times it will seem easy:

1. Cut off the tips of the wings and fold the first section of the wings under the second section.

2. Lay a long piece of cotton string (about 3 feet long) the length of a cutting board, and place the bird on its back with the cavity toward you on top of it, with the string just under the tail.

3. Cross the string over the legs, then cross the string under the ends of the drumsticks. Fold the tail up into the cavity and pull on the string to tighten it.

4. Draw each end of the string along the sides of the bird toward the breast, and pull on the strings while pushing the breast end of the bird toward you with your thumbs to make the bird as rounded in shape as possible.

5. Turn the bird breast-side down, bringing each end of the string over each wing and over the neck bone, tucking the neck skin under it; tie the two ends together tightly in a knot.

**Butterflying Whole Birds:** Butterflying ensures that a bird will lie on the grill as flatly as possible, so that it cooks evenly and makes an elegant presentation on the serving plate.

1. Cut off the wing tips. Place the bird on its side on a cutting board and cut in half through the backbone with a sharp knife.

2. Pull open the two halves of the bird and cut away and remove the backbone.

3. With the bird skin-side down on the cutting board, pound it several times with a heavy bottle to flatten it.

4. Cut off the protruding shoulder bones at the joint. Fold the first wing sections up and over backwards so that they point down toward the tail of the bird. Cut out and remove the breastbone.

5. Cut partially through the flesh of the bird where the thighs join the drumstick. (This allows this portion of the bird to cook faster.)

6. Make a small incision in the loose skin between the thigh and the breast on both sides of the bird; push the ends of the drumsticks through the holes.

The technique of butterflying is a refinement; you may prefer to simply cut birds in half for grilling. If so, you should cut off the backbone and trim the wing tips—the first step helps the bird to grill a little more evenly, and the second is a nicety. (If you want to make the bird lie as flat as possible on the grill without taking the trouble to butterfly it, you can simply flatten it by force: Cut the bird in half and remove the backbone. Place each half on a sturdy surface, top with a cutting board, and push on it with both hands until it is flattened.)

**Boning Whole Breasts:** We prefer boned whole breasts with the skin still attached for grilling, as they cook more evenly and are less likely to dry out than half breasts with or without bones. Most butcher shops will bone whole breasts for you, but you can also do it quite easily at home:

1. Place the whole breast, skin-side down, on a cutting board, with the pointed end at the top.

2. Using a sharp, narrow boning knife (or a paring knife if you have to), make a lengthwise cut through the white cartilage in the center of the breast.

3. Pick up the breast and bend the flesh away from the cartilage to make the fan-shaped keel bone pop out.

4. With your fingers, loosen the meat around this bone and the attached cartilage, then pull out the keel bone and cartilage.

5. With your knife, cut under the long bone that runs from the tip of each breast toward the center, pulling the flesh away from the bone and the rib cage as you cut. Repeat on the second side.

6. Cut out and remove the upside-down V of the wishbone on the end of breast facing you by cutting as close to the bone as possible.

## Secrets of the Grill: A Little Guide to Grilling Chicken and Other Birds

Our basic grilling philosophy for chicken and other birds is simple: Sear the bird quickly over a red-hot fire, then cover the grill for the remainder of the cooking time. Take care not to overcook; grilled birds should be crisp and brown on the outside, tender and juicy within. After removing the bird from the grill, cover it with aluminum foil and let it sit for a few minutes to settle the juices in the flesh (like most grilled foods, birds also will achieve their maximum flavor when warm or at room temperature, not hot off the grill). Adhering to this general philosophy, plus attention to the following specific details, will guarantee you superior grilled birds and make it easy to come up with your own dishes and variations on the recipes in this book.

• Use fresh-smelling, fresh-looking birds, and try to buy naturally raised birds whenever possible.

• Observe the cleanliness guidelines in the section "Cooking Chicken and Other Birds Safely," page 26.

• Use a marinade or a spice paste to help season the bird or, at the very least, rub the bird all over with oil before grilling. (When marinating, avoid uncoated aluminum or cast-iron containers, as the acid content of the marinade can interact with the metal to create a metallic taste. Use glass, ceramic, enameled cast iron, coated aluminum, or stainless steel.)

- Use boned whole chicken and duck breasts with skin, not half breasts.

- Make sure the bird is at room temperature.

- Learn to identify a red-hot fire. Too hot a fire will give a bird a burned outside and a dried-out interior.

- Keep the cooking rack clean.

- Frequent basting helps the bird stay juicy. Baste the bird every time it is turned, both before and after turning.

- Always cover the grill for cooking the bird after the initial searing or browning.

- Use an indirect fire for whole birds.

- Time the cooking of the bird carefully, using a kitchen timer—it's easy to lose track of time, especially when grilling for a group.

- Learn the guidelines for doneness (see "Cooking Times and Judging Doneness," page 18). When in doubt, or if you're a beginning grill cook, use an instant-read thermometer.

- Cover the bird with aluminum foil and let sit for 10 minutes at room temperature or in a very low oven for up to 20 minutes after grilling.

## SPECIAL INGREDIENTS

**Asian sesame oil:** A little sesame oil goes a long way. The lightest touch of this condiment made from toasted sesame seeds is enough to give a smoky Far East taste to marinades for chicken and other birds.

**Balsamic vinegar:** This all-purpose wine vinegar derives its name not from anything to do with balsam wood, but because it was prized for many years in Italy as a medicinal balm, or *balsamo,* perhaps because of its mellow, comforting taste. (Vinegar traditionally has been used in many countries of the world as a medicine and as a poultice.) Produced in Modena, Italy, balsamic vinegar has a deeply sweet and rich flavor, the result of long aging in wood casks. Use this versatile ingredient in any number of salad dressings, in simple vinaigrettes, as a flavor enhancer for strawberries and other fruits, and as an inspired addition to marinades for vegetables, birds, and other foods to be grilled. (To make a simple marinade for grilled vegetables, combine balsamic vinegar with extra-virgin olive oil and salt and pepper to taste; add fresh herbs if you like.)

**Chicken broth:** In an ideal world, we would all make our own chicken stock; in the real world, we'll settle for canned low-salt chicken broth. When grilling whole birds, however, we find something like an earthly paradise by cooking the giblets and any trimmings in a small saucepan of lightly salted water to cover for 30 minutes or longer. The resultant broth can be reduced by boiling to make just the right amount of rich liquid to add to a sauce for the bird, or to pass at the table by itself.

**Chilies:** The range of chilies is so large and varied that cooking with them can seem intimidating to the novice. The solution is simply to plunge in and start using chilies; they will open up an entirely new dimension in your cooking.

In this book we use both dried and fresh chilies in marinades and salsas. Dried chilies are usually soaked in warm water to cover for at least 2 hours or up to 8 hours; then they are drained and puréed, with a little of the soaking liquid, in a blender or food processor. They add an incomparable depth and richness to any sauce.

Fresh chilies need to be handled with care; either wear rubber gloves or make sure to wash your hands in hot soapy water right after working with them. Remove the seeds, the hottest part, if you're worried about the eventual heat of your sauce or marinade.

Chilies, both fresh and dried, vary widely in their degree of heat, both among different varieties and among individual chilies of the same variety. Like good grilling, good cooking with chilies is a matter of experimenting and paying attention to detail.

**Fish sauce:** This salty, savory sauce is used in Thailand, Cambodia, Laos, and Vietnam in the same way as soy sauce is used in China and Japan. Although it may be an acquired taste, it is acquired quickly and can become

addictive. Fish sauce is an excellent ingredient for marinades, and, combined with chopped green chilies, a little sugar, and chopped fresh cilantro, it makes an all-purpose dipping sauce that is especially good with grilled birds and fish.

**Garlic:** We use lots of garlic in our marinades, as we think it adds interest and complexity to most dishes. Use fresh garlic, not dried or powdered, which has an artificial taste. To simplify the peeling and chopping of garlic, use a large chef's knife to cut off the root end of each clove, then smash the cloves flat with the flat side of the knife blade; this makes the skins easy to remove. Chop the cloves by using the French technique of holding the tip of the knife down on the board with your left hand (if you are right handed) while moving the handle up and down and from left to right with your right hand to chop the cloves evenly. Keep a paring knife at hand to scrape the chopped garlic off the chef's knife periodically.

**Ginger:** The taste of fresh ginger is incomparable, but ginger root is hard to keep. Even in the refrigerator, it will soften and grow moldy after a couple of weeks. The best solution is to freeze the whole piece of ginger. To use, chop off a piece about the length you think you will use, then mince it with a sharp chef's knife. (You can peel it if you like, but it's not absolutely necessary for most of the recipes in this book.) An even easier method is simply to grate as much of the whole root as the recipe calls for. If you feel like going to more trouble, you can chop the ginger into pieces about 1 inch thick, peel each piece, and put them all into a jar with dry sherry to cover. Keep the jar in the refrigerator, and use the sherry as a replacement for Shao hsing wine, below.

**Herbs:** We like to use fresh herbs when we can, although we have given the three-to-one ratio of fresh to dried herbs in most of our recipes. The texture of fresh herbs is really only essential when the herbs are used in ingredients and as garnishes; dried herbs work perfectly well when they are reconstituted by being added to a marinade or sauce. In some cases, as for herb rubs to be spread over fish or birds before grilling, dried herbs are preferable.

When using fresh herbs, make sure that you strip the leaves or sprigs from the stems and chop only the leaves.

The stems are often too woody in texture and may also be bitter, as in the case of parsley stems.

**Hoisin sauce:** Add this sweet-spicy Asian sauce to barbecue sauces and marinades. As a marinade ingredient, it will add an attractive reddish color to grilled foods. Mix *hoisin* sauce with rice vinegar, Asian sesame oil, and a touch of sugar to make a simple dip or sauce for grilled birds.

**Hot chili oil:** You will find bottles of this orange-colored oil in Asian markets and in the specialty sections of many supermarkets. Use a dash whenever you want to add a light touch of heat to any dish.

**Hot chili paste:** Made primarily of chilies, salt, oil, and sometimes garlic, bottled chili paste can be found in Asian markets and many large supermarkets. Keep hot chili paste on hand in your refrigerator to use any time you want to add heat and depth to a sauce, marinade, or stir-fry. Chili pastes that contain soybeans are usually called hot bean pastes.

**Plum sauce:** Another Asian product; use this sweet fruit mixture in barbecue sauces and fruit-based marinades and sauces.

**Raspberry vinegar:** Raspberry vinegar adds its deeply sweet, fruity taste to salad dressings for bitter greens, salads with fruit or root vegetables, and marinades for wild game and such strongly flavored birds as duck and geese.

**Rice vinegar:** A wide variety of Asian vinegars, ranging from brown rice vinegar (look for this in natural foods stores) to Chinese black vinegar, are sometimes called "rice wine vinegar" because they are alcohol based. They are generally light and fresh, and may be used to balance stronger flavors and bring out the flavor of delicate foods. Try rice vinegar on grilled vegetables, as a marinade ingredient for chicken and fish, and as the acid ingredient in a subtle salad dressing.

**Shallots:** A great addition to many sauces and marinades, shallots are milder and sweeter than onions. Peel off the outer skin and chop them in the same manner as garlic, above.

**Shao hsing rice wine:** A sweet, mellow wine to add to marinades, it is widely available in Asian markets. Dry sherry is a good substitute.

**Soy sauce:** We use a low-salt soy sauce, available in natural foods stores.

**Zest:** The French distinguish between the *zeste* and the *zist* of citrus fruits, and with good reason: The *zeste* is the thin, colored exterior layer, whose oils contain the intense flavor of the fruit; the *zist* is its bitter white undercoat. Whenever a recipe calls for zest, make sure that you grate only the exterior layer of the citrus fruit and don't go through to the white portion. You can also strip off the zest with a potato peeler or a zester, then mince the zest finely with a chef's knife.

Chapter 3

# Grilling Recipes for Chicken and Other Birds

# TOM'S ASIAN-STYLE DRUMETTES

*Tom's Asian-style Drumettes · Grilled Chicken Sausages with a Selection of Mustards · Bruschette
Grilled Baby Leeks or Green Onions · Grilled Marinated Shrimp in the Shell · Chicory Salad · Cold Beer or Gamay Beaujolais*

*Serves 6 to 8 as a snack or part of an appetizer dinner*

A mix of Asian ingredients results in a hot, vibrant-flavored marinade. We've used drumettes because they're easier to eat and they cook more evenly, but chicken wings can also be used. You can find drumettes already cut in most supermarkets, or make your own by cutting off the wing joints of chicken wings, saving these sections to use in making home-made chicken broth.

Serve these spicy morsels as a snack or appetizer, or as part of a dinner consisting of grilled appetizers: Try grilled chicken sausages with a selection of mustards, grilled garlic bread, grilled baby leeks or green onions, and grilled marinated shrimp in the shell. Serve with a chicory salad and cold beer or Gamay Beaujolais.

## Marinade

⅓ cup low-salt soy sauce
⅓ cup Shao hsing wine or dry sherry
⅓ cup peanut oil
1 tablespoon plum sauce
1 tablespoon hot chili paste
3 garlic cloves, minced
1 tablespoon minced fresh ginger

2 to 3 pounds chicken drumettes
Fresh cilantro sprigs for garnish

In a small bowl, combine the ingredients for the marinade. Pour into a shallow non-aluminum baking dish and marinate the drumettes for 30 minutes to 1 hour at room temperature, or cover and refrigerate for 1 to 2 hours, turning the chicken 3 or 4 times during this time period.

Light a charcoal fire in a grill with a cover. If the drumettes have been refrigerated, remove them from the refrigerator 30 minutes before grilling.

Place the drumettes over a red-hot fire, baste with the marinade (using a brush, if possible), cover, and cook for 10 minutes. Baste and turn the drumettes, baste again, cover the grill, and cook for 5 to 6 minutes, or until they are well browned all over (cut one open to make sure it's opaque throughout).

Transfer the drumettes from the grill to a serving plate, cover them with aluminum foil, and let sit at room temperature for 10 minutes or in a very low oven for up to 20 minutes. Serve garnished with cilantro.

# GRILLED CHICKEN BREASTS WITH WHOLE-GRAIN MUSTARD SAUCE

*Grilled Chicken Breasts with Whole-Grain Mustard Sauce · Fresh Asparagus
Bulgur Pilaf · Light Amber Beer or Chardonnay*

*Serves 4*

The mustardy marinade gives boned whole chicken breasts a deep golden color and is reduced to make an intensely flavored sauce with overtones of amber beer and shallots. Serve with fresh asparagus, bulgur pilaf, and light amber beer or a Chardonnay.

## Marinade

    **2 large shallots, minced**
    **6 tablespoons whole-grain mustard**
    **½ cup amber beer**
    **½ cup unfiltered apple juice**
    **1 teaspoon brown sugar**
    **1 tablespoon olive oil**
    **Salt and pepper to taste**

    **3 boned whole chicken breasts with skin**
    **¼ cup amber beer**
    **½ cup homemade or canned low-salt chicken broth**

In a small bowl, combine the marinade ingredients. Pour into a shallow non-aluminum baking dish, add the chicken breasts, and marinate them for up to 1 hour at room temperature, or cover and marinate for at least 2 hours in the refrigerator, turning the breasts 3 or 4 times during this time period.

Light a charcoal fire in a grill with a cover. If the breasts have been refrigerated, remove them from the refrigerator at least 30 minutes before you plan to grill them.

When the fire is red hot, place the chicken on the grill, skin-side down, and cook for 4 minutes. Baste with the marinade, turn, baste again, and cook for 4 minutes on the second side. Baste, turn, and baste again; cover the grill and cook for 4 minutes. Baste, turn, and baste again; cover the grill and cook the breasts 4 more minutes (a total of 16 minutes), or until they are well browned on both sides and the meat is opaque throughout.

Transfer the breasts from the grill to a plate, cover them with aluminum foil, and let sit at room temperature for 10 minutes or in a very low oven for up to 20 minutes.

Meanwhile, pour the leftover marinade into a small saucepan, add the ¼ cup beer and chicken broth, and boil for several minutes until the mixture is reduced to a thick sauce. Stir the juice from the chicken plate into the sauce. Serve the warm chicken breasts on a pool of sauce, or with the sauce poured over them.

# WHOLE GRILL-ROASTED CHICKEN STUFFED WITH WILD RICE AND SHIITAKE MUSHROOMS

*Whole Grill-roasted Chicken Stuffed with Wild Rice and Shiitake Mushrooms*
*Grilled Whole Garlic Bulbs · Green Salad · Grilled Country Bread · Zinfandel*

*Serves 4*

Grill-roasted chicken is good anytime, but we especially like to serve this dish in autumn. Fresh rosemary and a savory stuffing of wild rice and *shiitake* mushrooms give the chicken a rich flavor that is complemented by the mysterious, smoky fragrance of charcoal. Serve with a fresh green salad, grilled slices of country bread drizzled with olive oil, and a Zinfandel.

## Stuffing

**½ pound (1 cup) wild rice, preferably lake harvested**
**4 cups water**
**½ teaspoon salt**
**8 large *shiitake* mushrooms or white cultivated mushrooms**
**3 tablespoons butter**
**1 tablespoon olive oil**
**4 green onions, chopped**

**One 3½- to 4-pound frying chicken, at room temperature**
**6 fresh rosemary sprigs, or 12 fresh thyme sprigs**
**Salt and pepper to taste**
**2 or 3 whole garlic bulbs**
**Rosemary or thyme sprigs for garnish**

To start the stuffing, soak the wild rice in cold water to cover for 30 minutes to 1 hour, or until the grains begin to open; drain. Pour the 4 cups water into a large saucepan, add the salt, and bring to a slow boil. Add the rice and cook, uncovered, for 30 minutes. Drain the rice in a sieve and let it cool.

Meanwhile, light a charcoal fire in a grill with a cover, using extra charcoal for the longer cooking time.

Cut the mushrooms crosswise into ⅛-inch-thick slices with the stems still attached. Melt 1 tablespoon of the butter in a medium sauté pan or skillet, add the oil, and sauté the mushrooms for about 10 minutes, or until they are golden brown.

In a small skillet, melt the remaining 2 tablespoons of the butter and sauté the green onions for a few minutes until they are tender. Add the drained wild rice and sautéed green onions to the sautéed mushrooms and mix well.

Loosen the skin of the chicken by slipping your index finger between the skin and the flesh of the breast, thighs, and legs. Place 1 sprig of rosemary or 2 sprigs of thyme under the skin over each leg, thigh, and breast half. Lightly salt and pepper the cavity of the chicken and stuff it loosely with the wild rice mixture. Truss the bird with cotton string as described on page 27. Set aside some of the herb sprigs for garnish, and soak the remaining leaves, stems, and sprigs in water to cover.

Place the chicken over a red-hot fire and sear it on all sides, turning carefully so as not to tear the skin; this should take about 5 minutes. Push the coals to one side of the grill and place a drip pan under the chicken. Turn the chicken breast-side down, with one side facing the coals, and place the whole garlic bulbs over the coals. Cover the grill, close the vents about half way, and cook the chicken for 20 minutes. Turn the garlic bulbs over and turn the chicken 180 degrees so that the other side faces the coals. Drain the soaked herbs and sprinkle them over the coals. Cook for another 20 minutes with the grill covered.

Turn the chicken breast-side up, cover, and cook for 10 minutes (a total of 55 minutes). Test the chicken for doneness by inserting a thermometer in the inside of the thigh; also check the temperature of the stuffing. The internal temperature of the meat should be 180°, and the temperature of the stuffing should reach 165°; this might take up to 10 minutes longer. Remove the garlic from the grill when the bulbs are soft all over.

Transfer the chicken from the grill to a plate. Cover with aluminum foil and let sit at room temperature for 10 minutes or in a very low oven for up to 20 minutes.

Just before serving, grill slices of country bread on both sides until browned; drizzle lightly with olive oil. To serve the chicken, cut and remove the trussing string, and carve and serve the chicken with the stuffing and garlic bulbs as a garnish, or carve at the table.

To eat the garlic, cut the root end off of the individual cloves and squeeze the sweet roasted garlic pulp onto the grilled bread.

# GRILLED CHICKEN BREASTS WITH APRICOT, RAISIN, AND MARSALA SAUCE

*Grilled Chicken Breasts with Apricot, Raisin, and Marsala Sauce · Sautéed Green Beans*
*Couscous with Pistachio Nuts · Sauvignon Blanc or Hot Mint Tea*

*Serves 4*

The tender meat of boned whole chicken breasts is paired with a nutty-sweet sauce of Marsala and dried fruits based on a reduction of the marinade. Serve this dish with sautéed green beans and couscous with pistachio nuts. To drink: Sauvignon Blanc or hot mint tea.

## Marinade

½ cup dry Marsala
2 tablespoons olive oil
8 to 10 whole dried apricots
2 tablespoons golden raisins
Salt and white pepper to taste

2 boned whole chicken breasts with skin
½ cup homemade or canned low-salt chicken broth
½ cup dry Marsala
Mint sprigs for garnish (optional)

In a small bowl, combine all of the marinade ingredients and pour into a shallow non-aluminum baking dish. Add the chicken breasts and marinate at room temperature for 1 to 2 hours, or cover and marinate for 2 to 4 hours in the refrigerator, turning the chicken 3 or 4 times during this time period.

Light a charcoal fire in a grill with a cover. If the chicken breasts have been refrigerated, remove them from the refrigerator at least 30 minutes before grilling.

Place the chicken breasts, skin-side down, over red-hot coals and cook for 4 minutes. Baste, turn, and baste again; cook for 4 minutes on the second side. Baste, turn, and baste again; cover and cook for 4 minutes. Baste, turn, and baste again; cover and cook for 4 minutes on the second side (a total of 16 minutes), or until the flesh is opaque throughout when cut into with a knife.

Transfer the chicken from the grill to a plate and cover with aluminum foil. Let sit at room temperature for 10 minutes or in a very low oven for up to 20 minutes.

Meanwhile, pour the remaining marinade with its fruit into a medium saucepan, add the ½ cup chicken broth and ½ cup Marsala, and boil over medium heat for about 5 minutes, or until reduced to a rich sauce.

Stir the juice from the chicken plate into the sauce. Serve the chicken on a pool of sauce or with the sauce poured over, garnished with mint sprigs, if you like.

# MESQUITE-SMOKED CHICKEN BREASTS WITH POBLANO-TOMATILLO SAUCE

*Mesquite-smoked Chicken Breasts with Grilled Poblano-Tomatillo Sauce*
*Black Bean Salad · Chilaquiles · Mexican Beer or Fresh Limeade*

*Serves 4*

This earthy Mexican dish is flavored with mesquite smoke and served with a picante sauce made with charred *poblano* chilies and *tomatillos*. Try to find these black-green triangular-shaped chilies with their hot, complex flavor, but if they're not available, use Anaheims, green bells, or any other large fresh green pepper. The fresh *tomatillos* can be replaced with canned *tomatillos* if necessary. Serve this dish with a black bean salad and *chilaquiles,* a casserole of tortilla strips and Monterey jack cheese. To drink: Mexican beer or fresh limeade.

**1 cup mesquite chips**
**4 fresh *poblano* chilies or other large fresh green chilies**
**10 fresh unhusked *tomatillos***
**    or drained canned *tomatillos***
**2 boned whole chicken breasts with skin**
**Oil for coating chicken**
**Salt and pepper to taste**
**¼ cup or more homemade or canned**
**    low-salt chicken broth**
**1 tablespoon olive oil**
**3 tablespoons chopped fresh cilantro**
**Salt to taste**
**Cilantro sprigs for garnish**

Light a charcoal fire in a grill with a cover. Soak the mesquite chips in water to cover for 30 minutes before grilling.

As soon as the coals are evenly lighted, place the whole *poblanos* and unhusked fresh *tomatillos* on the cooking rack and sear them on all sides for 15 to 20 minutes, or until well charred all over. Transfer them from the grill to a plate. Place the chilies in a small paper bag. Set the *tomatillos* and chilies aside to cool at room temperature.

Meanwhile, when the coals are red hot, coat the chicken breasts all over with olive oil, sprinkle with salt and pepper, and place, skin-side down, on the cooking rack to cook for 4 minutes. Turn and cook on the second side for 4 minutes.

Drain the mesquite chips and sprinkle them evenly over the coals. Brush the chicken with olive oil, turn the chicken, and brush the second side with oil. Cover the grill, partially close the vents, and cook the chicken for 4 minutes. Brush the chicken with olive oil, turn, and brush the second side with oil. Cover and cook 4 minutes longer (a total of 16 minutes), or until the flesh is opaque throughout when cut into with a knife.

Transfer the chicken from the grill to a plate, cover with aluminum foil, and let sit at room temperature for 10 minutes or in a very low oven for up to 20 minutes.

Meanwhile, make the sauce: Remove and discard the *tomatillo* husks and stems and place the grilled *tomatillos* (or drained canned *tomatillos*) in a blender or food processor. Remove the chilies from the paper bag and open them to remove and discard the stems and seeds. With your fingers, rub off as much of the charred skin as possible; it's okay to leave a little—it adds to the taste of the sauce. Don't rinse the chilies under water, as this reduces the flavor. Add the peeled chilies, chicken broth, 1 tablespoon oil, chopped cilantro, and salt to the blender or food processor and puree to a smooth sauce (add more broth if necessary). Adjust the seasoning.

Pour the juice from the chicken plate into the sauce and blend. Pour a pool of sauce onto a serving plate and place the chicken breasts on top of the sauce. Pour the remaining sauce into a small bowl. Garnish the chicken with cilantro sprigs and serve the chicken accompanied with the bowl of sauce.

# GRILLED CARIBBEAN CHICKEN

*Grilled Caribbean Chicken · Grilled Parsnips or Plantains · Braised Mustard Greens*
*Fresh Mango Chutney · Jamaican Beer*

*Serves 4*

This chicken gets its heat from bottled Caribbean chili sauce, a fiery substance made from the Scotch bonnet chili. We've given you a range of the amount of hot sauce to use, depending on your tolerance of heat. Sometimes called "jerk" or "jerked" chicken, this dish can also be made with a marinade using a mixture of dried spices sold as jerk spice mix. (Supposedly, the term *jerk* comes from the jerking motion with which barbecued foods—presumably ribs—are eaten.)

Grilled sliced plantains are a traditional side dish in the islands (choose plantains with a thoroughly black skin), but we also like the nutty taste of grilled sliced parsnips. Other good companions are braised mustard greens and a fresh mango chutney (use the recipe for Fresh Nectarine Chutney on page 81, substituting 1 mango for the nectarines). To drink: Jamaican beer.

## Marinade

2 to 3 tablespoons Caribbean hot chili sauce
Juice of 1 orange
6 tablespoons chopped fresh basil, or
    2 tablespoons crumbled dried basil
6 tablespoons chopped fresh thyme, or
    2 tablespoons crumbled dried thyme
2 tablespoons minced fresh parsley
1 tablespoon Dijon mustard
1 tablespoon dry mustard
1 tablespoon white vine vinegar
Salt to taste

4 chicken thighs with legs, or 8 thighs
Basil and/or thyme sprigs for garnish (optional)

In a small bowl, combine all the ingredients for the marinade. Pour the marinade into a shallow non-aluminum baking dish. Add the chicken and marinate for 1 to 2 hours at room temperature, or cover and marinate for 2 to 4 hours in the refrigerator, turning the chicken 3 or 4 times during this time period.

Light a charcoal fire in a grill with a cover. If the chicken has been refrigerated, remove it from the refrigerator 30 minutes before grilling.

When the fire is red hot, place the chicken, skin-side down, on the cooking rack and cook for 4 minutes. Baste with the marinade, turn, and baste again; cover and cook for 10 minutes. Baste, turn, and baste again; cover and cook for 5 minutes. Baste, turn, and baste again; cover and cook for 5 minutes on the second side (a total of 24 minutes), or until the juices run clear when a thigh is pierced with a knife.

Transfer the chicken from the grill to a plate, cover with aluminum foil, and let sit at room temperature for 10 minutes or in a very low oven for up to 20 minutes. Serve garnished with fresh herbs, if you like.

# VINE-SMOKED CHICKEN BREASTS WITH HERBS AND MUSTARD-CREAM SAUCE

*Vine-smoked Chicken Breasts with Herbs and Mustard-Cream Sauce · Grilled Halved Red Potatoes*
*Grilled Red Onion Wedges and Grilled Sliced Zucchini with Balsamic Vinegar · Chardonnay*

*Serves 4*

We think of this as a perfect end-of-summer meal: chicken breasts perfumed with the fragrance of fresh herbs and the winey smoke from grapevine cuttings. Because they are boned and rolled, the chicken breasts make an elegant presentation, and they are complemented by a creamy sauce based on a reduction of the wine and herb marinade. Serve them with grilled halved red potatoes; grilled red onion wedges and grilled zucchini slices sprinkled with balsamic vinegar; and a steely California Chardonnay.

**4 boned whole chicken breasts with skin**
**2 bunches fresh oregano or thyme**
**½ cup olive oil**
**1 cup dry white wine**
**4 medium shallots, chopped**
**Salt and pepper to taste**
**1 cup grapevine cuttings**
**1 cup homemade or canned low-salt chicken broth**
**½ cup half-and-half**
**½ teaspoon Dijon mustard**

Loosen the skin of the chicken breasts slightly and place about 6 herb sprigs under the skin on each side of each whole breast. Turn the breasts skin-side down.

Chop enough herb leaves to make about ¾ cup of chopped herbs, reserving any leftover sprigs, stems, and leaves. Sprinkle about 2 tablespoons of chopped herbs evenly over each whole breast. Turn in the bottom and top inch or so of each breast, then roll the breast from one side to make a compact bundle. Tie each breast several times both crosswise and lengthwise with white cotton string.

In a small bowl, combine the olive oil, wine, shallots, the remaining 4 tablespoons chopped herbs, salt, and pepper, and pour into a large non-aluminum bowl. Add the rolled chicken breasts and marinate at room temperature for 30 minutes to 1 hour, or cover and refrigerate for 1 to 2 hours, turning the chicken 3 or 4 times during this time period.

Light a charcoal fire in a grill with a cover. Place the grapevine cuttings in cold water to cover and let soak for 30 minutes before grilling. Reserve a few of the herb sprigs for garnish, and place the remaining herb leaves, sprigs, and stems in water to cover. If the chicken has been refrigerated, remove it from the refrigerator 30 minutes before grilling.

Place the rolled chicken breasts on the cooking rack over a red-hot fire and sear on all sides for a total of 5 minutes, basting several times with the marinade. Drain the grapevine cuttings and sprinkle them evenly over the coals. Baste the chicken, cover, partially close the vents, and cook for 15 minutes.

Baste, turn, and baste the chicken again. Drain the herb leaves, spigs, and stems and sprinkle them over the coals. Cover the grill and cook the chicken 10 minutes longer (a total of 30 minutes), or until the flesh is opaque throughout when cut into with a knife, or a thermometer inserted into the center of a breast reaches 170°.

Transfer the chicken from the grill to a plate, cover with aluminum foil, and let sit at room temperature for 10 minutes or in a very low oven for up to 20 minutes.

Meanwhile, pour the leftover marinade into a small saucepan and boil on the stove for 3 to 5 minutes, or until the liquid is reduced to a thick syrup; watch carefully and stir occasionally, so it doesn't burn. Whisk in the chicken broth and half-and-half and boil again for 3 to 5 minutes, or until the mixture is reduced to the consistency of heavy cream; whisk in the mustard.

Remove the strings from the chicken bundles and cut each one crosswise into ¼-inch-thick slices. Whisk any juices from the chicken plate into the sauce. Pour a puddle of sauce onto the plate, arrange the chicken slices over the sauce, garnish the plate with herb sprigs, and serve.

# GRILL-ROASTED CHICKEN WITH CORN BREAD STUFFING

*Grill-roasted Chicken with Corn Bread Stuffing · Braised Swiss Chard*
*Grilled Tomato Halves · Sauvignon Blanc*

*Serves 4 to 5*

Sage, prosciutto, and white wine add their flavors to this satisfying, savory grill-roasted chicken. The stuffing recipe makes twice as much as is needed to fill the bird, so you can bake the extra stuffing separately. (Buy packaged unseasoned corn bread crumbs, or use leftover corn bread as an excuse to make this dish.) Serve with braised Swiss chard, grilled tomato halves, and a Sauvignon Blanc.

**One 4½- to 5-pound roasting chicken**

## Marinade

⅓ cup dry white wine
⅓ cup olive oil
3 tablespoons chopped fresh sage, or
   1 tablespoon chopped dried sage leaves
Salt and pepper to taste

## Corn Bread Stuffing

2 large shallots, minced
1 tablespoon butter
1 tablespoon olive oil
3 tablespoons chopped fresh sage, or
   1 tablespoon chopped dried sage leaves
2 cups unseasoned dried corn bread crumbs
   (packaged or homemade)
⅔ cup or more rich homemade chicken broth or
   reduced canned low-salt chicken broth
⅓ cup dry white wine
2 ounces thin-sliced prosciutto, cut into thin slivers
Salt and pepper to taste

Fresh sage sprigs for garnish (optional)

Reserve the giblets from the chicken to freeze for later use, or place them in a small saucepan with lightly salted water to cover. Cook over low heat for 30 minutes or longer; strain and reduce to make a rich broth. Use as part or all of the chicken broth for the stuffing.

In a small bowl, combine all the ingredients for the marinade. Pour into a large non-aluminum bowl. Add the whole chicken and marinate at room temperature for 1 to 2 hours, or cover and refrigerate for 2 to 4 hours, turning the chicken 3 or 4 times during this time period.

Light a charcoal fire in a grill with a cover, using extra charcoal to allow for the long cooking time. If the chicken has been refrigerated, remove it from the refrigerator 1 hour before stuffing and grilling.

To make the stuffing: In a small skillet, sauté the shallots in butter and oil until translucent; add the sage and stir. Remove the pan from the heat and let sit for 4 or 5 minutes. Pour the corn bread crumbs into a large bowl, stir in the shallot mixture, then stir in the chicken broth and the white wine. Add the prosciutto, stirring to blend it evenly into the stuffing; season to taste.

Drain the chicken, place it on a cutting board, and stuff loosely with the stuffing (the stuffing may seem dry, but it will gain moisture as the bird cooks). Close the cavity and truss the bird as described on page 27.

Sear the bird on all sides over red-hot coals—this will take a total of about 5 minutes. (Take care during searing, as the alcohol in the wine may cause flare-ups.)

Push the coals to one side of the grill and place a drip pan on the other side of the fuel grate. Position the chicken, breast-side down, on the cooking rack over the drip pan, with one side of the breast facing the fire. Baste the chicken with the marinade, cover the grill, and cook for 20 minutes. Baste the chicken again and turn it 180 degrees so that the other side of it is toward the fire. Cover the grill and cook for another 20 minutes.

Meanwhile, bake the remaining stuffing: Add a little more chicken broth to the remaining stuffing until it is well moistened. Place the stuffing in a small buttered baking dish and bake in a preheated 325° oven until heated through, about 20 minutes. Remove from the oven and keep warm until serving.

Baste the chicken and turn it breast-side up. Baste again, cover, and cook the chicken for another 10 minutes (a total of 1 hour and 15 minutes). Test for doneness (a thermometer inserted in the inside of the thigh should register 180°, and the stuffing should register 165°); you may need to cook the bird as much as 10 minutes longer at this point.

Transfer the chicken from the grill to a serving plate, cover with aluminum foil, and let sit at room temperature for 10 minutes or in a very low oven for up to 20 minutes. Slice and serve with the stuffing as a garnish around the edge of the serving plate, or carve at the table. Garnish with sprigs of fresh sage, if you like.

# GRILLED QUAIL WITH LEEKS

*Grilled Quail with Leeks · Risotto or Grilled Polenta*
*Mesclun Salad · Nebbiolo*

*Serves 8 as a first course, 4 to 6 as a main course*

Like other game birds, quail can be delivered to your doorstep twenty-four hours after you've ordered them by telephone. We've given instructions for both boned and unboned quail; boned are preferable, if you can find them, as they are easier to eat. To help boned quail keep their shape, they should be lightly stuffed with a simple stuffing. Each stuffed quail then can be cut in half to serve.

We planned this dish as a first course, but you also could serve it as a main course with risotto or grilled polenta and a salad of *mesclun* (mixed baby bitter greens). In either case, these quail are delicious served with a Nebbiolo wine.

**6 leeks, trimmed to leave about 3 inches of green part**
**One 1-inch piece fresh ginger, peeled and cut into**
**    thin slices**
**Zest of 1 orange, cut into strips**
**Juice of 2 oranges**
**⅓ cup low-salt soy sauce**
**⅓ cup safflower oil**
**1 tablespoon honey**
**1 teaspoon rice vinegar**
**Ground white pepper to taste**
**Dash Asian sesame oil**
**8 boned or unboned quail**
**Corn Bread Stuffing, page 50, made without**
**    prosciutto, or about 2 cups of a simple stuffing**
**    of your choice (if you are using boned quail)**
**Homemade or canned low-salt chicken broth for**
**    oven-baked stuffing (optional)**

In a large skillet or sauté pan, blanch the leeks in boiling water for about 5 minutes. Drain and let cool. Reserve 3 of the leeks. To make the marinade, cut the remaining 3 leeks into 1-inch pieces.

In a small bowl, combine the cut-up leeks, ginger, orange zest and juice, soy sauce, oil, honey, rice vinegar, pepper, and sesame oil. Pour into a large non-aluminum bowl. Marinate the quail at room temperature for 30 minutes to 1 hour, or cover and marinate in the refrigerator for 1 to 2 hours, turning the quail 3 or 4 times during this time period.

Prepare a charcoal fire in a grill with a cover. If the quail have been refrigerated, remove them from the refrigerator at least 30 minutes before grilling.

Meanwhile, if you are using boned quail, prepare the corn bread stuffing or a stuffing of your choice and use it to fill the quail loosely. (Place any leftover stuffing in a buttered baking dish, add a little extra chicken broth, and bake in a preheated 325° oven for 25 minutes, or until warmed through.) Add the reserved whole leeks to the marinade.

Place the quail over a red-hot fire and brown them all over, turning and basting them with the marinade several times, for a total of 5 minutes. Watch them carefully to keep them from burning; if the fire seems too hot, allow it to burn down slightly, or move the coals apart a little to lower the heat. Place the whole leeks on the grill and baste them with the marinade.

Baste the quail, turn them breast-side down, and baste again; cover the grill and cook them for 3 minutes if they are boned, and 5 minutes if they are not. Baste and turn the quail, and baste the quail and the leeks; cover the grill and cook another 3 minutes for boned quail and 5 minutes for bone-in quail (a total of 11 minutes for boned quail and 15 minutes for bone-in quail), or until the juice from a thigh runs clear when pierced with a knife.

Transfer the quail from the grill to a serving plate, cover with aluminum foil, and let sit at room temperature for 10 minutes or in a very low oven for up to 20 minutes. Cut the whole leeks into strips lengthwise and place on a serving plate to make a bed for the quail. Place the quail on top of the leeks to serve.

# HOT FOURTH-OF-JULY BARBECUED CHICKEN

*Hot Fourth-of-July Barbecued Chicken* · *Grilled Unpeeled Potato Wedges*
*Shredded Red and Green Cabbage in Vinaigrette* · *Light Amber Beer or Ale*

*Serves 4 to 6*

We've updated the classic American barbecue sauce with Asian ingredients to give it a little more complexity. This recipe makes a thick, sweet-hot sauce to spread over mesquite-smoked grilled chicken. Serve with grilled unpeeled potato wedges and shredded red and green cabbage in vinaigrette.

## Hot Fourth-of-July Barbecue Sauce

    5 bacon slices
    2 tablespoons oil
    2 large garlic cloves, minced
    1 cup catsup
    ⅓ cup red wine vinegar
    1 medium onion, chopped
    1 cup dry red wine
    1 teaspoon Worcestershire sauce
    2 tablespoons *hoisin* sauce
    1 tablespoon hot chili paste
    Fresh lemon juice to taste
    Salt and pepper to taste

    2 frying chickens, cut in half and backbones removed
    1 cup apple wood chips

To make the barbecue sauce: In a small skillet, cook the bacon over medium-low heat until it is crisp; remove the bacon to paper towels to drain. In a medium saucepan, heat the oil and sauté the garlic until it is translucent. Add the catsup, vinegar, onion, red wine, Worcestershire sauce, *hoisin* sauce, and chili paste to the saucepan. Crumble the bacon and add it to the sauce. Add lemon juice, salt, and pepper to taste.

Reserving a small amount of sauce to brush over the chicken, place the saucepan over low heat, cover, and let the sauce cook for 1 to 2 hours to develop the flavors, stirring occasionally.

Meanwhile, light a charcoal fire in a grill with a cover. Brush the chicken lightly with the reserved barbecue sauce mixture. Let the chicken sit at room temperature for at least 30 minutes before grilling. Soak the apple wood chips in cold water to cover for at least 30 minutes before grilling.

Place the chicken halves on the cooking rack over red-hot coals and sear them on both sides for a total of about 5 minutes. Drain the apple chips and sprinkle them evenly over the coals. Turn the halves bone-side down, cover the grill, partially close the upper vents, and cook for 30 minutes. Turn the halves skin-side down and cook for another 5 minutes (a total of 40 minutes), or until the juices run clear when a thigh is pierced with a sharp knife, or a thermometer inserted in the inside of a thigh reaches 175° to 180°.

Turn the chicken, brush with the cooked barbecue sauce, turn it skin side down again, cover, and cook for another 2 to 5 minutes, or until the sauce browns and glazes the chicken.

Transfer the chicken from the grill to a plate and cover it with aluminum foil. Let the chicken sit at room temperature for 10 minutes or in a very low oven for up to 20 minutes. Pour the juices from the chicken plate into the barbecue sauce. Pour the sauce into a bowl, and serve the sauce alongside the chicken.

# THAI-STYLE GRILLED POUSSINS WITH PEANUT SAUCE

*Thai-style Grilled Poussins with Peanut Sauce · Sticky Rice*
*Grilled Green Onions · Thai Beer*

*Serves 4*

Tender young chickens are marinated in a piquant mixture of Thai tastes, then grilled and served with a savory peanut sauce. The delicate, juicy flesh of *poussins* is an interesting contrast with this combination of ingredients, but if you can't find *poussins,* use 2 small fryers or 4 Cornish hens. Serve with sticky rice, grilled green onions, and Thai beer.

If you can't find the tiny, hot, green Thai chilies, use the thicker and larger green *jalapeños.* Remember to wear rubber gloves or to wash your hands in hot soapy water right after handling the chilies. The peanut sauce recipe makes about 1½ cups, and leftover sauce will keep in the refrigerator for up to a week. Try it as a sauce for grilled vegetables, grilled fish, and chicken salad.

## Marinade

- Juice of 2 limes
- 2 tablespoons Thai fish sauce
- 3 tablespoons low-salt soy sauce
- 1 shallot, minced
- ⅓ cup peanut oil
- 3 to 5 green Thai chilies, or 1 to 3 *jalapeño* chilies, minced (leave the seeds in for a hotter sauce)

2 *poussins*

## Peanut Sauce

- ¼ cup peanut oil
- ½ cup smooth peanut butter
- 1 tablespoon minced fresh ginger
- 2 garlic cloves, minced
- 1 tablespoon dried red pepper flakes
- 1 tablespoon low-salt soy sauce
- Juice of 1 lime
- 2 tablespoons rice vinegar
- ½ cup homemade or canned low-salt chicken broth
- Leaves from ½ bunch fresh cilantro, minced

- ½ teaspoon honey, or to taste
- Salt to taste

Cilantro sprigs for garnish

In a small bowl, combine the ingredients for the marinade and pour it into a large non-aluminum bowl. Add the *poussins* and marinate them at room temperature for 1 to 2 hours, or cover and refrigerate for 2 to 3 hours, turning them 3 or 4 times during this time period.

Light a charcoal fire in a grill with a cover. If the *poussins* have been refrigerated, remove them from the refrigerator 45 minutes before grilling.

Meanwhile, prepare the peanut sauce: Place all of the ingredients in a blender or a food processor and blend to a smooth sauce. Adjust the seasoning and set aside.

Place the *poussins* over a red-hot fire and sear on all sides for 5 minutes. Push the coals into a loose circle, place a drip pan in the center, and position the *poussins,* breast-side up, in the center of the cooking rack over the drip pan.

Cover the grill and cook the birds for 10 minutes, then baste with the marinade, re-cover the grill, and cook them 5 minutes longer. Baste the birds again, turn them breast-side down, baste again, re-cover the grill, and cook them 20 minutes longer (a total of 40 minutes), or until they are well browned and the juices run clear when the thighs are pierced with a knife (or until a thermometer inserted into the inside of a thigh reads 180°).

Transfer the *poussins* from the grill to a plate, cover them with aluminum foil, and let sit at room temperature for 10 minutes, or place in a very low oven for up to 20 minutes. Blend the juice from the plate into the sauce. Serve the *poussins* on a pool of sauce, or pass a bowl of sauce at the table. Garnish the *poussins* with cilantro sprigs.

# CHICKEN FAJITAS

*Chicken Fajitas · Fresh Salsa · Guacamole · Grilled Whole Poblano Chilies Stuffed with Goat Cheese*
*Corn or Flour Tortillas · Mexican Beer or Margaritas*

*Serves 4 to 6*

Grilled marinated chicken, cut into strips and served with tortillas and salsa, is the latest dish from Mexico to be adopted wholeheartedly in this country. Our marinade has the extra kick of tequila, and the chicken breasts are grilled whole to keep them juicy. If you like the taste of mesquite wood, add mesquite chips to the coals.

Serve with a fresh salsa of onions, tomatoes, and *jalapeños;* guacamole with lots of lemon juice and garlic; hot corn or flour tortillas; and grilled *poblano* chilies stuffed with goat cheese. To drink: Mexican beer or Margaritas.

## Marinade

Juice of 2 limes
½ cup tequila
2 tablespoons olive oil
½ cup chopped onion
2 tablespoons chopped fresh cilantro
Salt to taste

2 boned whole chicken breasts with skin
1 cup mesquite chips (optional)
12 corn or 6 flour tortillas
Cilantro sprigs for garnish

In a small bowl, combine the ingredients for the marinade and pour into a shallow non-aluminum baking dish. Add the chicken breasts and marinate at room temperature for 30 minutes to 1 hour, or cover and refrigerate for 1 to 2 hours, turning the chicken 3 or 4 times during this time period.

Light a charcoal fire in a grill with a cover. If the chicken breasts have been refrigerated, remove them from the refrigerator 30 minutes before grilling. If you are using mesquite chips, soak them in cold water to cover for 30 minutes before grilling.

When the fire is red hot, moisten your hands by dipping them in water and lightly dampen both sides of each tortilla by running your wet hands over it. Place the tortillas in a stack on a large square of aluminum foil. Close the packet tightly and place it on one side of the cooking rack.

Place the chicken breasts, skin-side down, over the red-hot fire, and cook for 4 minutes. Baste with the marinade, turn, and baste again; cook for 4 minutes on the second side.

If you are using mesquite chips, drain them and sprinkle them evenly over the coals. Baste the chicken, turn, and baste again; cover the grill (partially close the vents if you are using mesquite chips) and cook the breasts for 4 minutes. Turn over the packet of tortillas. Baste, turn, and baste the chicken breasts again; cover the grill and cook the chicken for 4 minutes on the second side (a total of 16 minutes), or until the meat is opaque throughout when cut into with a knife.

Transfer the chicken from the grill to a plate, cover with aluminum foil, and let sit for 10 minutes at room temperature. Check the tortillas to make sure they are not drying out; when they are heated through, remove them from the grill, keeping them hot inside the foil. Slice the chicken breasts into inch-thick slices, mound them on a serving plate, garnish with cilantro sprigs, and serve at once alongside the hot tortillas, salsa, and guacamole.

# GRILLED MEDITERRANEAN CHICKEN

*Grilled Mediterranean Chicken · Grilled Potato Slices*
*Green Salad · Sliced Tomatoes with Balsamic Vinegar · Bruschette · Chianti Classico*

*Serves 3 to 4*

The marinade for this dish simmers down into a chunky sauce like a cooked salsa, which is delicious as a topping for *bruschette,* the original garlic bread: slices of country bread grilled, rubbed with cut garlic, and drizzled with olive oil. Other good companions for this oregano-scented chicken are grilled potato slices, a green salad, and the summer's ripest tomatoes, sliced and anointed with balsamic vinegar. To drink: Chianti classico.

If you can't find flavorful vine-ripened tomatoes for this marinade, look for ripe Roma tomatoes or use cherry tomatoes, which usually have a good flavor.

## Marinade

½ cup olive oil
⅓ cup balsamic vinegar
1 medium onion, chopped
6 garlic cloves, minced
1 large ripe tomato, chopped
¼ teaspoon dried red pepper flakes
1 tablespoon chopped fresh oregano,
   or 1 teaspoon crumbled dried oregano
2 tablespoons chopped fresh parsley
Salt and pepper to taste

1 frying chicken, cut into serving pieces
Oregano or parsley sprigs for garnish (optional)

In a small bowl, combine the ingredients for the marinade. Pour half of the marinade into a shallow non-aluminum baking dish, reserving the remaining half. Add the chicken to the baking dish and marinate at room temperature for 30 minutes to 1 hour, or cover and marinate for 2 to 4 hours in the refrigerator, turning the chicken 3 or 4 times during this time period.

Light a charcoal fire in a grill with a cover. If the chicken has been refrigerated, remove it from the refrigerator at least 30 minutes before grilling.

Place the chicken pieces, skin-side down, over a red-hot fire and sear for 2 minutes. Baste with the marinade, turn, baste again, and sear the chicken for 2 minutes on the second side. Baste, turn, and baste the chicken again, and cook uncovered for 2 to 3 minutes. Baste, turn, and baste again; cover the grill and cook the chicken for 6 minutes. Baste, turn, and baste again; cover the grill and cook the chicken for 5 or 6 minutes on the second side (a total of 17 to 19 minutes), or until the skin is well browned on both sides and the meat is opaque throughout when cut into with a knife.

Transfer the chicken from the grill to a plate, cover with aluminum foil, and let sit at room temperature for 10 minutes or in a very low oven for up to 20 minutes.

Meanwhile, place the reserved marinade in a small saucepan and simmer until it is reduced to a thick sauce, about 10 minutes. Add the juices from the chicken plate to the sauce. Coat the chicken with the sauce, or pass the sauce in a bowl to accompany the chicken or to spread on *bruschette*. Garnish the chicken with herb sprigs, if you like.

# TANDOORI CHICKEN KABOBS

*Tandoori Chicken Kabobs · Basmati Rice Pilaf with Saffron*
*Fresh Cilantro Chutney · Garlic Nan · Beer*

*Serves 4*

Tandoori spice mix gives the chicken a rich rust color and a dusky, spicy flavor, while the yogurt in the marinade tenderizes the kabobs to an almost buttery texture. This dish is a good choice for the kamado, which is so similar to the clay *tandoor* oven that gives its name to this type of Indian cuisine. The kabobs may also be cooked over a medium-hot fire in a covered metal grill with partially closed vents; the cooking time will be slightly shorter. Serve the kabobs with basmati rice pilaf with saffron, a fresh cilantro chutney, garlic *nan,* and beer.

**4 boned chicken breast halves**

## Marinade

½ **cup plain yogurt**
**2 tablespoons oil**
**Juice of 1 lime**
½ **medium onion, chopped**
**3 large garlic cloves, chopped**
**2 tablespoons tandoori spice mix**
**Salt to taste**

**Lime wedges and cilantro sprigs for garnish**

Soak 4 long wooden skewers in water to cover for 15 minutes. Remove the skin from the chicken breasts and cut each breast into thirds crosswise. Thread the chicken pieces lengthwise on the 4 skewers and place the skewers in a shallow non-aluminum baking dish.

In a small bowl, combine the marinade ingredients. Spoon the marinade over the chicken to cover all the pieces. Marinate at room temperature for 1 to 2 hours, or cover and marinate in the refrigerator for 2 to 4 hours, turning the skewers 3 or 4 times during this time period.

Light a charcoal fire in a kamado or a grill with a cover. If the chicken has been refrigerated, remove it from the refrigerator 30 minutes before grilling.

Place the skewers on the cooking rack over a medium-hot fire and cook for 5 minutes. Baste with the marinade, turn, and baste again; cook for 5 minutes on the second side. Baste, turn, and baste again. Cover the kamado or grill, partially close the vents, and cook for 10 minutes. Baste, turn, and baste again; cover and cook for 5 more minutes, or until the chicken is opaque but still juicy when cut into with a knife (a total of about 25 minutes in a kettle grill and a few minutes longer in a kamado).

Transfer the kabobs from the grill to a plate, cover with aluminum foil, and let sit at room temperature for 10 minutes or in a very low oven for up to 20 minutes. To serve, garnish with lime wedges and cilantro sprigs.

# HICKORY-SMOKED WHOLE CHICKEN WITH KANSAS CITY BARBECUE SAUCE

*Hickory-smoked Whole Chicken with Kansas City Barbecue Sauce · Grilled Sweet Potatoes*
*Creamy Coleslaw · Corn Bread · Beer, Iced Tea, or Lemonade*

*Serves 2 to 3*

Real barbecue is the result of long, slow cooking over a wood fire in a pit or a brick oven, and is best suited to large cuts of beef or pork. But your covered grill can be used as a smoke oven for chicken and other birds by using an indirect fire and water-soaked hardwood chips. The kamado is even better for smoke-roasting, as it provides the same kind of convection heating as a brick oven or a cooking pit does.

We use a quick homemade spice mix to rub on the chicken before grilling; this gives the cooked chicken a beautiful, deep brownish red coat. Serve with creamy coleslaw, corn bread, and beer, iced tea, or lemonade.

## Kansas City Barbecue Sauce

   2 tablespoons olive oil
   5 to 6 garlic cloves, minced
   1 large white onion, minced
   3 ripe large tomatoes, chopped
   2 tablespoons chopped fresh basil, or
      2 teaspoons crumbled dried basil
   3 tablespoons tomato paste
   ⅔ cup distilled white vinegar
   2 tablespoons bourbon
   ¾ teaspoon salt
   2 tablespoons brown sugar
   2 teaspoons Worcestershire sauce
   ½ teaspoon Tabasco sauce, or to taste
   2 to 3 shakes cayenne, or to taste
   2 to 2½ cups water

## Spice Rub

   1 tablespoon ground cumin
   ½ teaspoon cayenne
   1 teaspoon paprika
   1 teaspoon salt
   1 teaspoon ground black pepper
   1 teaspoon brown sugar

   One 3½-pound whole chicken
   1 cup hickory chips
   Fresh basil sprigs for garnish (optional)

One day ahead, or at least 2 hours before serving, prepare the barbecue sauce: In a large skillet or sauté pan, heat the olive oil and sauté the garlic and onion until translucent. Add the chopped tomatoes and cook, uncovered, over medium heat, stirring occasionally, for

about 30 minutes, or until the mixture thickens. Add the basil, tomato paste, vinegar, and bourbon and cook again, uncovered, over medium heat for about 15 minutes, stirring occasionally. Add the salt, brown sugar, Worcestershire sauce, Tabasco sauce, and cayenne, and 1½ cups of the water. Reduce the heat to low, cover, and simmer, stirring occasionally and adding the remaining water as needed, for 1 to 1½ hours, or until the sauce is thick and rich, and the flavors are well blended. Adjust the seasoning.

In a small bowl, combine all of the ingredients for the spice rub. Rub the whole chicken thickly and well all over with the spice rub, using all of it. Let the chicken sit at room temperature for at least 30 minutes or up to 1 hour, or cover and let sit in the refrigerator for up to 2 hours.

Light a charcoal fire in a grill with a cover, using extra charcoal to allow for the long cooking time. If the chicken has been refrigerated, remove it from the refrigerator 45 minutes before grilling. Soak the hickory chips in water to cover for 30 minutes before grilling.

Place the chicken over red-hot coals and sear on all sides for a total of about 5 minutes. Drain the hickory chips and sprinkle them evenly over the coals. Move the chicken to one side of the cooking grill and turn it breast-side down, with one side facing the coals. Drain the hickory chips and sprinkle them evenly over the coals. Cover the grill, partially close the vents, and cook the chicken for 20 minutes. Turn the chicken 180 degrees so that the other side faces the coals, cover the grill, and cook another 20 minutes. Turn the chicken breast-side up, cover the grill, and cook up to another 20 minutes (a total of about 1 hour), or until the juice runs clear when the thigh is pierced with a knife, or a thermometer inserted in the inside of a thigh reads 180°.

Transfer the chicken from the grill to a plate and cover with aluminum foil. Let sit at room temperature for 10 minutes or in a very low oven for up to 20 minutes. Warm the barbecue sauce if you like (it can also be served at room temperature), and stir the juices from the chicken plate into the sauce. Serve the chicken garnished with basil sprigs, if you like, and accompanied with the barbecue sauce.

# GRILLED BONED TURKEY BREAST
# STUFFED WITH EMMENTHALER CHEESE AND PROSCIUTTO

*Grilled Boned Turkey Breast Stuffed with Emmenthaler Cheese and Prosciutto*
*Potato Pancakes · Watercress Salad with Orange Slices · Chardonnay*

*Serves 4 to 6*

A boned half turkey breast is easy to grill because it cooks evenly, and it's easy to serve. Savory layers of prosciutto and melted cheese make this dish an elegant choice for a company dinner. This is a good recipe to multiply for feeding a large group, and it's a perfect choice for grilling in a kamado. Any leftovers will make great sandwiches. Serve with a watercress salad with orange slices, potato pancakes, and Chardonnay.

**One 3- to 4-pound boned half turkey breast**
**¼ pound thinly sliced prosciutto**
**¼ pound thinly sliced Emmenthaler cheese**

## Marinade

**1 cup dry white wine**
**Juice of 1 lemon**
**1 medium onion, chopped**
**1 tablespoon Dijon mustard**
**6 tablespoons chopped fresh marjoram, or**
  **2 tablespoons crumbled dried marjoram**
**1 teaspoon paprika**
**Salt and freshly ground black pepper**

**Sprigs of marjoram for garnish (optional)**

Using a sharp slicing knife and beginning at the point of the breast, make a deep cut down the center of the breast, leaving about 1 inch of the breast intact at the bottom of the cut. Insert several slices of prosciutto. Top this with several slices of cheese. Repeat until the prosciutto and cheese are used up. Close the opening with vertically placed wooden toothpicks.

In a small bowl, combine all the ingredients for the marinade and pour into a large non-aluminum bowl. Add the turkey breast and let it marinate at room temperature for 30 minutes to 1 hour, or cover and marinate in the refrigerator for 1 to 2 hours, turning the turkey 3 or 4 times during this time period.

Light a charcoal fire in a grill with a cover or a kamado. If the turkey has been refrigerated, remove it from the refrigerator and let it sit at room temperature for 1 hour before grilling.

Place the turkey breast, skin-side down, on the cooking rack over red-hot coals and sear for 3 to 4 minutes. Baste, turn, and baste again. Move the turkey breast to one side of the cooking rack, cover, and cook for 20 minutes on a kettle or console grill, and a few minutes longer in a kamado, or until a thermometer inserted in the turkey breast reaches 170°.

Transfer the turkey breast to a plate, cover it with aluminum foil, and let sit at room temperature for 10 minutes or in a very low oven for up to 20 minutes.

To serve, remove the toothpicks and cut the turkey breast into crosswise slices ¼ to ½ inch thick. Garnish with marjoram sprigs to serve, if desired.

# GRILLED PHEASANT WITH A SAUCE OF MUSHROOMS, CREAM, AND BRANDY

*Grilled Pheasant with a Sauce of Shiitake Mushrooms, Cream, and Brandy*
*Soft Polenta with Parmesan Cheese · Steamed Broccoli with Lemon Juice · Pinot Noir*

*Serves 2*

The sauce is a classic of French cuisine, but is paired here with pheasant perfumed with the flavor of the grill. Any mushroom, domestic or wild, can be used in this sauce, but we prefer the intense flavor of the *shiitake*. You might want to try fresh *porcini* (also called *cèpes*). This makes a fine autumn dinner served with a soft polenta with lots of grated Parmesan cheese stirred in, steamed broccoli with fresh lemon juice, and a Pinot Noir.

**One 2¼-pound pheasant (with giblets if possible)**

## Marinade

**1 large shallot, minced**
**⅓ cup good brandy**
**⅓ cup olive oil**
**3 teaspoons chopped fresh thyme, or**
  **1 teaspoon crumbled dried thyme**
**Salt and pepper to taste**

## Sauce

**1 tablespoon butter**
**1 tablespoon olive oil**
**1 shallot, minced**
**¼ pound *shiitake* mushrooms, sliced (about 2 cups)**
**2 tablespoons brandy**
**⅓ cup half-and-half**
**½ cup reserved pheasant broth or rich chicken broth**

**Fresh thyme sprigs for garnish (optional)**

Reserve the pheasant giblets if you have them. Cut the pheasant in half alongside the backbone; cut out the backbone and reserve it.

In a small bowl, combine all the ingredients for the marinade and pour into a large non-aluminum bowl. Add the pheasant to the marinade and marinate at room temperature for 1 to 2 hours, or cover and refrigerate for 2 to 4 hours, turning the pheasant 3 or 4 times during this time period.

Meanwhile, place the reserved giblets and the pheasant backbone in a small saucepan, cover with lightly salted water, and simmer for 30 minutes. Strain through a sieve and return the broth to the pan. Cook at a slow boil over medium heat until the liquid has reduced to a richly flavored broth; you should have about ½ cup. Set aside.

Light a charcoal fire in a grill with a cover. If the pheasant has been refrigerated, remove it from the refrigerator at least 30 minutes before grilling.

Sear the pheasant on each side over red-hot coals for a total of 4 to 5 minutes, then baste it with the marinade. Turn the halves bone-side down, baste again, cover the grill, and cook for 10 minutes. Baste, turn, and baste again; cover the grill and cook for 10 more minutes. Baste, turn, and baste again; cover and cook up to 10 minutes longer (a total of 25 to 35 minutes), or until the juice runs clean when a thigh is pierced with a knife, or a thermometer inserted in the inside of a thigh reads 180°.

Meanwhile, to start the sauce, heat the butter and oil to bubbling in a medium skillet or sauté pan. Add the shallot and sauté for 2 or 3 minutes, or until translucent. Add the sliced mushrooms and sauté for about 8 minutes, or until golden brown; set aside.

Transfer the pheasant from the grill to a serving plate and cover with aluminum foil while finishing the sauce (it may also be kept in a very low oven for up to 20 minutes).

While the pheasant is resting, finish the sauce: Add the brandy to the sautéed mushrooms and boil over high heat for 2 to 3 minutes to cook off the alcohol. Add the half-and-half and about ¼ cup of broth. Cook at a slow boil over medium heat until the liquid has reduced to the consistency of thick cream; taste and adjust the seasoning with salt, pepper, and fresh lemon juice, adding more broth if you like.

Pour the juices from the pheasant plate into the sauce. Serve the pheasant halves in a pool of sauce, or with the sauce poured over, or pass the sauce in a bowl. Garnish the serving platter with thyme sprigs, if you like.

# Smoked Sesame Chicken on a Bed of Bitter Greens

*Smoked Sesame Chicken on a Bed of Bitter Greens · Grilled Fennel Slices*
*Grilled Beet Slices · Green Onion Pancakes · Moselle or Riesling*

*Serves 4*

This chicken gets its smoky taste from mesquite charcoal, mesquite wood chips, and toasted sesame oil, assertive flavors that are balanced by the bitter greens. The marinade is reduced slightly and served as a warm dressing for the chicken and the greens. Serve with grilled sliced fennel, grilled sliced beets, and green onion pancakes. To drink: a Moselle or a Riesling.

## Marinade

- 1 tablespoon chopped fresh ginger
- 2 tablespoons chopped shallots
- 2 teaspoons Asian sesame oil
- 3 tablespoons low-salt soy sauce
- 1 tablespoon sesame seeds
- ¼ teaspoon hot chili oil
- ¼ cup peanut oil
- ⅓ cup rice vinegar

- 2 boned whole chicken breasts with skin
- 1 cup mesquite wood chips
- 4 to 6 cups mixed bitter greens such as chicory, *radicchio, frisée, arugula,* and endive
- 1 tablespoon sesame seeds for garnish

In a small bowl, combine all the ingredients for the marinade and pour into a shallow non-aluminum baking dish. Place the chicken breasts in the dish and marinate at room temperature for 1 to 2 hours, or cover and place in the refrigerator for 2 to 4 hours.

Light a charcoal fire in a grill with a cover. If the chicken has been refrigerated, remove it from the refrigerator 30 minutes before grilling. Soak the mesquite chips in water to cover for 30 minutes before grilling.

When the coals are red hot, place the chicken, skin-side down, on the cooking rack and cook for 4 minutes. Baste with the marinade, turn, and baste again; cook for 4 minutes on the second side.

Drain the mesquite chips and sprinkle them over the coals. Baste the chicken, turn, and baste again; cover the grill, partially close the vents, and cook the breasts for 4 minutes. Baste, turn, and baste again; cover the grill and cook for 4 minutes on the second side (a total of 16 minutes), or until the breasts are well browned on both sides and the flesh is opaque throughout when cut into with a knife.

Transfer the chicken from the grill to a plate and cover it with aluminum foil. Let sit at room temperature for 10 minutes or in a very low oven for up to 20 minutes.

To serve, make a bed of the bitter greens on a serving plate. Cut the chicken breasts into long narrow slices and lay them on top of the greens. Pour the remaining marinade into a small saucepan and boil over medium-high heat until the liquid is slightly reduced. Pour the juice from the chicken plate into the reduced sauce. Pour the sauce over the sliced chicken and the bitter greens. Sprinkle with sesame seeds and serve at once.

# CAJUN-STYLE GRILLED CHICKEN

*Cajun-style Grilled Chicken · Braised Mustard Greens*
*Spoon Bread or Grilled Cornmeal Mush · Cold Beer*

*Serves 4*

The Cajun spice mixes now on the market add a new zest to foods for the grill, especially chicken and other birds. The blend we use combines black pepper, garlic, thyme, and red pepper. The onion rings add flavor to the marinade and then are grilled over low coals as a garnish for the chicken. Serve with braised mustard greens, spoon bread or grilled cornmeal mush, and cold beer.

## Marinade

Juice of 2 lemons (about ½ cup)
¼ cup olive oil
2 tablespoons Cajun spice mix
2 to 4 dashes Tabasco sauce
2 large yellow onions, sliced and separated into rings

2 boned whole chicken breasts with skin

In a small bowl, combine the ingredients for the marinade and pour into a shallow non-aluminum baking dish. Add the chicken breasts and marinate for 30 minutes to 1 hour at room temperature, or cover and marinate for 1 to 2 hours in the refrigerator, turning the chicken 3 or 4 times during this time period.

Light a charcoal fire in a grill with a cover. If the chicken has been refrigerated, remove it from the refrigerator 30 minutes before grilling.

Place the chicken, skin-side down, over a red-hot fire, baste with the marinade, and grill for 4 minutes. Baste, turn, and baste again, and grill the chicken on the second side for 4 minutes.

Using tongs, remove the onion rings from the marinade and place them on a grilling grid (or a piece of metal screening) to one side of the grill. Baste, turn, and baste the chicken again; cover the grill and cook the chicken for 4 minutes. Baste, turn, and baste the chicken. Turn the onions, cover the grill, and cook the chicken and onions for 4 minutes, or until the chicken is opaque throughout when cut into with a knife. (The chicken will take a total of about 16 minutes to cook.)

Transfer the chicken from the grill to a plate, cover with aluminum foil, and let sit at room temperature for 10 minutes or in a very low oven for up to 20 minutes. Let the onions continue to cook if necessary, turning them again, until they are well browned. Serve the grilled onion rings alongside the chicken as a garnish.

# CHINESE BARBECUED CHICKEN

*Chinese Barbecued Chicken · Chinese Noodle Salad
Grilled Japanese Eggplant · Chinese Beer or Gewürztraminer*

*Serves 4 to 6*

Basting with this tangy, sweet-hot marinade gives the chicken a shiny orange-red glaze. Use a little less chili paste to start with if you prefer a less spicy dish; add more plum sauce for a sweeter marinade. Plum sauce, rice wine, and hot chili paste are all available in Asian markets; low-salt soy sauce is available in many supermarkets and in natural foods stores. Serve this dish with a salad of Chinese egg noodles, grilled Japanese eggplant, and either Chinese beer or a Gewürztraminer.

## Marinade

**Cloves from 1 whole bulb of garlic, minced**
**1 tablespoon plum sauce**
**⅓ cup Shao hsing wine or dry sherry**
**1 tablespoon low-salt soy sauce**
**1 tablespoon hot chili paste, or to taste**

**2 or 3 boned whole chicken breasts with skin**
**Cilantro sprigs for garnish**

In a small bowl, combine the ingredients for the marinade. Place the chicken in a shallow non-aluminum baking dish and marinate at room temperature for up to 1 hour, or cover and place in the refrigerator for at least 2 hours. Turn the chicken 3 or 4 times during this time period.

Light a charcoal fire in a grill with a cover. If the chicken has been refrigerated, remove it from the refrigerator at least 30 minutes before grilling.

Place the chicken, skin-side down, over a red-hot fire and cook for 4 minutes. Baste with the marinade, turn, and baste again; cook for 4 minutes. Baste, turn, and baste again; cover and cook for 4 minutes. Baste, turn, and baste again; cover and cook for 4 minutes on the second side (a total of 16 minutes), or until the chicken is well browned on the outside and opaque throughout when cut into with a knife.

Transfer the chicken from the grill to a plate, cover with aluminum foil, and let sit at room temperature for 10 minutes or in a very low oven for up to 20 minutes. Serve garnished with cilantro sprigs.

# GRILLED BREADED CHICKEN THIGHS

*Grilled Breaded Chicken Thighs · Potato Salad*
*Grilled Corn with Butter and Lime Juice · Sauvignon Blanc or Iced Tea*

*Serves 4*

A recipe that combines the best of two worlds: the flavor of charcoal and the crisp coating of fried chicken. Serve this with your favorite potato salad and grilled corn with butter and fresh lime juice. To drink: Sauvignon Blanc or iced tea.

**1 cup flour**
**½ teaspoon salt**
**2 teaspoons paprika**
**2 eggs beaten with 2 teaspoons olive oil**
**8 chicken thighs, or 4 thighs with legs**
**1½ cups fresh bread crumbs made from country-style**
    **bread with crusts removed★**
**Parsley sprigs for garnish**

In a small bowl, combine the flour, salt, and paprika. Place the flour mixture on a plate, and place the beaten egg in a pie plate. Dip each piece of chicken in the flour to coat evenly, shaking off the excess, then into the egg mixture, shaking off the excess. Place the chicken in the bread crumbs and turn to coat evenly all over.

Place the chicken pieces in a baking pan lined with waxed paper, cover, and refrigerate for at least 30 minutes so that the crumbs will adhere to the chicken.

Meanwhile, light a charcoal fire in a grill with a cover. Remove the chicken from the refrigerator 15 minutes before grilling.

Cook the chicken over a red-hot fire for 4 minutes, then turn and cook for 4 minutes on the second side (turn carefully so as not to dislodge the coating). Turn the chicken, cover the grill, and cook for 5 minutes; turn again and cook for 5 minutes on the second side (a total of 18 minutes), or until the thighs are golden brown all over and the meat is opaque throughout when cut into with a knife.

Transfer the chicken from the grill to a plate. Cover the chicken loosely with aluminum foil and let sit at room temperature for 10 minutes or in a very low oven for up to 20 minutes. Serve garnished with parsley sprigs.

★To make fresh bread crumbs, tear the trimmed bread slices into large pieces and whirl them in a blender or food processor.

# GRILLED PORT-MARINATED CHICKEN WITH PRUNES

*Grilled Port-marinated Chicken with Prunes · Garlic Mashed Potatoes*
*Braised Spinach or Brussels Sprouts · White Burgundy*

*Serves 3 to 4*

Try this dish on a mild winter day. The deeply flavored marinade combines ingredients usually reserved for pork or game and cooks down into a dark, fruity sauce. Serve with garlic mashed potatoes, braised spinach or Brussels sprouts, and a white Burgundy.

## Marinade

**1 dozen pitted prunes**
**1 cup ruby port**
**½ cup dry sherry**
**4 garlic cloves, minced**
**1 tablespoon chopped fresh thyme, or**
  **1 teaspoon crumbled dried thyme**
**2 tablespoons olive oil**
**1 tablespoon honey**
**Pinch of salt**

**1 large whole fryer, cut in half and backbone removed**
**Thyme sprigs for garnish (optional)**

In a medium non-aluminum saucepan, soak the prunes in the port for 30 minutes. Add the remaining marinade ingredients to the pan. Pour half of the liquid into a large non-aluminum bowl (leaving the prunes in the pan), add the chicken, and marinate for 1 to 2 hours at room temperature, or cover and marinate for 2 to 4 hours in the refrigerator, turning the chicken 3 or 4 times during this time period.

Prepare a fire in a grill with a cover. If the chicken has been refrigerated, remove it from the refrigerator 30 minutes before grilling.

Sear the chicken on both sides over a red-hot fire for a total of 5 minutes. Baste with the marinade, turn bone-side down, and baste again; cover the grill and cook the chicken for 30 minutes. Baste, turn the chicken skin-side down, and baste again; cover and cook for another 5 minutes (a total of 40 minutes), or until the chicken is well browned and the juice runs clear when a thigh is pierced with a knife (or until a thermometer inserted in the inside of a thigh registers 180°).

Meanwhile, place the prunes and the reserved marinade over low heat to simmer until the sauce is thickened, about 20 minutes.

Transfer the chicken from the grill to a plate, cover with aluminum foil, and let sit at room temperature for 10 minutes or in a very low oven for up to 20 minutes. Stir the juice from the chicken plate into the sauce. Serve the chicken with the warm reduced sauce and whole prunes poured over. Garnish with thyme sprigs, if you like.

# GRILLED CHICKEN BREASTS IN YELLOW CURRY WITH NECTARINE CHUTNEY

*Grilled Chicken Breasts in Yellow Curry with Fresh Nectarine Chutney*
*Basmati Rice Pilaf with Aniseeds · Sautéed Sugar Snap Peas · Riesling*

*Serves 4*

The curry spices infuse the chicken with an intense yellow color that is beautifully balanced in appearance and taste by the fresh chutney. The chutney is colorful and refreshing, and the recipe works well with other fresh fruits in place of the nectarines, such as blueberries, mangoes, or apricots (it makes about 2 cups). Serve this dish with basmati rice pilaf with aniseeds, sautéed sugar snap peas, and a chilled Riesling.

## Marinade

⅓ cup vegetable oil
⅓ cup dry champagne or white wine
1 tablespoon grated fresh ginger
1 teaspoon ground turmeric
1 pinch saffron
1 teaspoon ground coriander
2 dashes cayenne
Salt to taste

2 boned whole chicken breasts with skin

## Fresh Nectarine Chutney

2 ripe nectarines, pitted and chopped
1 small red bell pepper, cored, seeded, and chopped
½ medium white or red onion, chopped
2 green onions, chopped
1 tablespoon minced fresh ginger
1 *jalapeño*, minced (with seeds)
1 garlic clove, minced
¼ cup white wine vinegar
1 tablespoon brown sugar
2 tablespoons minced fresh mint
1 tablespoon minced fresh cilantro
Salt to taste

Mint and/or cilantro sprigs for garnish

In a small bowl, combine all the ingredients for the marinade and pour it into a shallow non-aluminum dish. Add the chicken and marinate for 30 minutes to 1 hour at room temperature, or cover and refrigerate for up to 2 hours in the refrigerator, turning the chicken 3 or 4 times during this time period.

Light a charcoal fire in a grill with a cover. If the chicken has been refrigerated, remove it from the refrigerator at least 30 minutes before grilling.

Meanwhile, prepare the fresh chutney: In a medium ceramic or glass bowl, combine all the ingredients for the chutney and let sit at room temperature for 30 minutes to 1 hour to allow the fruit to macerate and the flavors to develop.

Place the chicken, skin-side down, over a red-hot fire and cook for 4 minutes. Baste with the marinade, turn, baste again, and cook the chicken for 4 minutes on the second side. Baste, turn, and baste the chicken again; cover and cook for 4 minutes. Baste, turn, and baste again; cover and cook 4 minutes longer on the second side (a total of 16 minutes), or until the chicken is well browned on both sides and is opaque throughout when cut into with a knife.

Transfer the chicken from the grill to a plate, cover with aluminum foil, and let sit at room temperature for 10 minutes or in a very low oven for up to 20 minutes. Garnish the serving plate with herb sprigs and serve the chutney alongside the chicken.

*Grilled Cornish Hens with Chili Butter and Grilled-Corn Salsa*
*Hot Flour Tortillas · Mexican Beer*

*Serves 4 to 6*

We use fresh Cornish hens for this dish, but you will find that chili butter is wonderful on any grilled bird, and on most grilled fish and meats, too. In fact, chili butter is great on almost anything, so you might want to make extra and freeze any that is left over. It will keep for about a week in the refrigerator and several months in the freezer. Look for dried New Mexican or *pasilla* chilies in Latino markets. New Mexican chilies are narrow, dark red, and about 6 inches long, while *pasillas,* which are dried *poblanos,* are black-red and triangular in shape.

The grilled-corn salsa makes a colorful, sweet-savory bed for the birds, which take on the deep orange-red color of their marinade. Serve with Mexican beer and hot flour tortillas.

## Chili Butter

**6 dried New Mexican or *pasilla* chilies**
**6 tablespoons butter, melted**
**Salt to taste**

**4 Cornish hens**

## Grilled-Corn Salsa

**4 ears of corn, shucked**
**Olive oil for brushing corn**
**1 ripe large tomato, chopped**
**½ medium red onion, chopped**
**2 tablespoons chopped fresh cilantro**
**1 tablespoon fresh lime juice, or to taste**
**Salt to taste**

**About ½ cup reserved Cornish hen broth or**
**    rich chicken broth**
**Cilantro sprigs for garnish**

Soak the whole dried chilies in warm water to cover for at least 2 hours or up to 8 hours. Remove the chilies from the water, reserving the liquid, and remove and discard the stems and seeds. Place the chilies in a blender or food processor with about ⅓ cup of the soaking liquid and blend to a smooth purée, adding more liquid if needed. Pour in the melted butter and blend until the mixture is well combined. Season to taste.

If you are using fresh Cornish hens, remove the giblets and reserve them. Place the hens in a deep glass or ceramic bowl. Reserve 1 cup of the chili butter to use

for sauce, and pour the remaining chili butter over the Cornish hens to coat them evenly. Marinate at room temperature for 1 to 2 hours, turning the birds 3 or 4 times during this time period (don't marinate in the refrigerator, as the butter in the sauce will harden).

Meanwhile, if you have Cornish hen giblets, place them in a small pan, add lightly salted water to cover, and simmer over a low fire for about 30 minutes. Remove the giblets and cook the liquid over medium heat for several minutes, until reduced to a rich broth. You should have ¼ to ½ cup of broth. Set aside.

Light a charcoal fire in a grill with a cover, using extra charcoal to allow for the longer cooking time. When the coals are red hot, brush the corn with olive oil and place it on the grill. Place the Cornish hens on the grill also, and turn the corn and the hens to brown the corn and sear the hens on all sides for a total of 5 minutes, basting the hens several times with the chili butter used for marinating. Remove the corn from the grill and let cool.

Place the hens, breast-side down, on one side of the cooking rack over a drip pan, with one side of the breast facing the coals. Baste with chili butter, cover the grill, and cook the hens for 20 minutes. Turn the hens 180 degrees so that they will cook on the other side, baste, re-cover the grill, and cook for 20 minutes on the second side.

Baste, turn the hens breast-side up, cover, and cook up to 20 minutes longer (a total of 65 minutes), or until the juices run clear when a thigh is pricked with a fork or a thermometer inserted in the inside of a thigh reads 180°. Transfer the hens from the grill to a plate and cover with aluminum foil; let sit for 10 minutes at room temperature or in a very low oven for up to 20 minutes.

Meanwhile, cut the kernels from the corn and place in a large bowl. Add the remaining salsa ingredients and adjust the seasoning. Make a bed of the salsa on a serving plate. In a small pan, heat the reserved chili butter and add enough broth to make a smooth sauce.

Pour the juices from the Cornish hen plate into the sauce. Place the hens on top of the bed of salsa and serve, garnished with sprigs of cilantro and accompanied with a bowl of the warm chili butter.

# Twice-grilled Duck Breast in a Raspberry Vinegar Marinade

*Twice-grilled Duck Breast in a Raspberry Vinegar Marinade*
*Grilled Sliced Turnips and Whole Baby Carrots · Arugula Salad with Extra-virgin Olive Oil · Bordeaux*

*Serves 4 to 6*

Duck breast has become popular in the last few years, and with good reason: The meaty breast with its thick layer of insulating fat is rich in taste, almost beeflike in texture, and grills beautifully, lending itself to a range of assertively flavored marinades. Here the extra-large whole breast of the Muscovy duck is marinated in a fruity mixture of raspberry vinegar and orange juice, grilled rare, then sliced and briefly grilled again. Serve with grilled sliced turnips or whole baby carrots; an *arugula* salad with a vinaigrette of extra-virgin olive oil; and a good Bordeaux.

Leftover grilled duck breast is a prized ingredient for salads of bitter greens and fruit (use a raspberry vinegar–based dressing); try sliced mangoes, ripe peaches or apricots, and/or fresh raspberries with red onion slices. Cold grilled duck breast is also good on dark bread with green onions and whole-grain mustard.

## Marinade

> ½ cup black or red raspberry vinegar
> ⅓ cup olive oil
> Juice of ½ orange
> 1½ teaspoons chopped fresh thyme, or
>    ½ teaspoon crumbled dried thyme
>
> One boned whole (2-pound) Muscovy
>    duck breast with skin
> Fresh raspberries or blackberries and
>    thyme sprigs for garnish (optional)

In a small bowl, combine all the ingredients for the marinade and pour into a shallow non-aluminum baking dish. Add the duck breast and marinate it for 1 to 2 hours at room temperature, or cover and refrigerate for 2 to 4 hours, turning the duck 3 or 4 times during this time period.

Light a charcoal fire in a grill with a cover. If the duck breast has been refrigerated, remove it from the refrigerator at least 30 minutes before grilling.

Sear the duck breast, skin-side down, over a red-hot fire for 5 minutes; watch for flare-ups, as the fat from the duck will burn and smoke. Baste with the marinade, turn, baste again, and sear the duck breast for 5 minutes on the second side. Baste, turn, and baste again; cover the grill and cook the duck skin-side down for 5 minutes. Baste, turn, and baste again; cover and cook another 5 minutes, or until well browned on the outside but medium-rare within (a total of 20 minutes).

Transfer the duck from the grill to a plate, cover it with aluminum foil, and let sit at room temperature for at least 10 minutes or in a very low oven for up to 20 minutes.

Cut the breast in half down the center, then cut it crosswise into ¼-inch-thick slices. Pour the juices from the plate into the marinade. Return the duck slices to the marinade for 3 or 4 minutes, then grill the slices again for 1 minute per side. (Use a grill basket or a grilling grid to keep the slices from falling through the cooking rack.)

Mound on a serving plate and serve garnished with berries and thyme sprigs, if you like.

**Variation:** Check the duck for doneness before removing it from the grill; you may want to cook it a little longer, as it is not grilled a second time in this variation; the flesh should remain medium-rare in the center, however. While the duck is resting under its aluminum foil, pour the remaining marinade into a small saucepan and boil over medium heat for several minutes until it is reduced to a syrupy sauce. Pour the juices from the duck plate into the sauce. Pool the sauce on a serving plate, slice the duck, and place the slices over the sauce. Garnish and serve. Or pour the sauce over the duck slices, or pass the sauce in a bowl at the table.

# MAIL-ORDER SOURCES

## Grills

HASTY-BAKE
7656 East 46th Street
Tulsa, OK 74145
800-4AN-OVEN
Charcoal console grills and
built-ins.

KAMADO
BSW, Inc.
4680 East Second Street
Benicia, CA 94510
707-745-8175
Ceramic grill-ovens in
several sizes.

KINGSFORD COMPANY
P.O. Box 24305
Oakland, CA 94623
800-537-2823
Charcoal kettle grills with
shelves, rack, and ash catcher.

THERMOS
Route 75
Freeport, IL 61032
800-435-5194
A wide range of gas console
grills with accessories.

WEBER
Weber-Stephen Products
Company
200 East Daniels Road
Palatine, IL 60067-6266
800-323-7598
Charcoal and gas kettle grills
in several sizes and styles;
grill accessories.

## Charcoal and Smoking Woods

CHARCOAL COMPANION
7955 Edgewater Drive
Oakland, CA 94621
510-525-3800 (in California),
or 800-521-0505;
fax 510-632-1986
A wide variety of smoking
woods.

DESERT MESQUITE OF
ARIZONA
3458 East Illini Street
Phoenix, AZ 85040
602-437-3135
Mesquite smoking woods.

HUMPHREY CHARCOAL
CORPORATION
P.O. Box 440
Brookville, PA 15825
814-849-2302
Hardwood lump charcoal
and hardwood charcoal
briquettes.

LAZZARI FUEL COMPANY
P.O. Box 34051
San Francisco, CA 94134
415-467-2970 (in California),
or 800-242-7265
Mesquite charcoal and
smoking woods.

LUHR JENSEN & SONS, INC.
P.O. Box 297
Hood River, OR 97031
503-386-3811 (in Oregon), or
800-535-1711
Smoking woods.

## Grilling Accessories

CHARCOAL COMPANION
7955 Edgewater Drive
Oakland, CA 94621
510-632-2100 (in California),
or 800-521-0505;
fax 510-632-1986
A wide variety of grill
accessories.

GRIFFO PRODUCTS
1400 North 30th
Quincy, IL 62301
800-426-1286
Grilling grids and grill
baskets.

OUTDOOR COMPANY
(O.D.C.)
P.O. Box 6255
Evansville, IN 47719-0255
800-544-5362
Accessories and replacement
parts for gas grills.

WEBER
Weber-Stephen Products
Company
200 East Daniels Road
Palatine, IL 60067-6266
800-323-7598
Accessories for kettle grills;
grilling tools.

## Naturally Raised Poultry and Game Birds

D'ARTAGNAN
399–419 St. Paul Avenue
Jersey City, NJ 07306
800-327-8246
Naturally raised chickens and
wild and farm-raised game
birds.

DURHAM–NIGHT BIRD
358 Shaw Road, No. A
South San Francisco, CA
94080
415-737-5873
Naturally raised chickens and
farm-raised game birds.

THE GAME EXCHANGE
(retail);
Polarica Game USA
(wholesale)
P.O. Box 880204
San Francisco, CA
94188-0204
415-647-1300 (in California),
or 800-GAME-USA
Wild and farm-raised game.

# BIBLIOGRAPHY

Editors of Time-Life Books. *Outdoor Cooking.* Alexandria, Va.: Time-Life Books, 1983.

Ellis, Merle. *Cutting Up in the Kitchen.* San Francisco: Chronicle Books, 1975.

Kilham, Christopher S. *The Bread and Circus Wholefood Bible.* Reading, Mass.: Addison-Wesley, 1991.

Pépin, Jacques. *La Technique.* New York: New York Times Book Co., 1976.

United States Department of Agriculture, Food Safety and Inspection Service. *Food News for Consumers,* vol. 8, no. 1 (spring 1991).

——. *Preventing Foodborne Illness: A Guide to Safe Food Handling.* Home and Garden Bulletin No. 247 (September 1990).

# LIST OF RECIPES *with Suggested Accompaniments*

**Grill-roasted Chicken with Corn Bread Stuffing**
Braised Swiss chard
Grilled tomato halves
Sauvignon Blanc

**Tom's Asian-style Drumettes**
Grilled chicken sausages with a
    selection of mustards
*Bruschette*
Grilled baby leeks or
    green onions
Grilled marinated shrimp
    in the shell
Chicory salad
Cold beer or Gamay Beaujolais

**Grilled Chicken Breasts with Whole-Grain Mustard Sauce**
Fresh asparagus
Bulgur pilaf
Light amber beer or Chardonnay

**Grilled Mediterranean Chicken**
Grilled potato slices
Green salad
Sliced tomatoes with
    balsamic vinegar
Chianti Classico

**Thai-style Grilled Poussins with Peanut Sauce**
Sticky rice
Grilled green onions
Thai beer

**Cajun-style Grilled Chicken**
Braised mustard greens
Spoon bread or grilled
    cornmeal mush
Cold beer

**Grilled Breaded Chicken Thighs**
Potato salad
Grilled corn with butter and
    lime juice
Sauvignon Blanc or iced tea

**Chicken Fajitas**
Fresh salsa
Guacamole
Grilled whole *poblano* chilies
    stuffed with goat cheese
Corn or flour tortillas
Mexican beer or Margaritas

**Hot Fourth-of-July Barbecued Chicken**
Grilled unpeeled potato wedges
Shredded red and green cabbage
    in vinaigrette
Light amber beer or ale

**Grilled Chicken Breasts in Yellow Curry with Fresh Nectarine Chutney**
Basmati rice pilaf with aniseeds
Sautéed sugar snap peas
Riesling

**Whole Grill-roasted Chicken Stuffed with Wild Rice and Shiitake Mushrooms**
Grilled whole garlic bulbs
Green salad
Grilled country bread
Zinfandel

**Grilled Quail with Leeks**
Risotto or grilled polenta
*Mesclun* salad
Nebbiolo

**Twice-grilled Duck Breast in a Raspberry Vinegar Marinade**
Grilled sliced turnips and whole
    baby carrots
*Arugula* salad with extra-virgin
    olive oil
Bordeaux

**Chinese Barbecued Chicken**
Chinese noodle salad
Grilled Japanese eggplant
Chinese beer or Gewürztraminer

**Grilled Caribbean Chicken**
Grilled parsnips or plantains
Braised mustard greens
Fresh mango chutney
Jamaican beer

**Grilled Cornish Hens with Chili Butter and Grilled-Corn Salsa**
Hot flour tortillas
Mexican beer

**Tandoori Chicken Kabobs**
Basmati rice pilaf with saffron
Fresh cilantro chutney
Garlic nan
Beer

**Grilled Pheasant with a Sauce of Shiitake Mushrooms, Cream, and Brandy**
Soft polenta with Parmesan
    cheese
Steamed broccoli with lemon
    juice
Pinot Noir

**Grilled Boned Turkey Breast Stuffed with Emmenthaler Cheese and Prosciutto**
Potato pancakes
Watercress salad with
    orange slices
Chardonnay

**Grilled Port-marinated Chicken with Prunes**
Garlic mashed potatoes
Braised spinach or
    Brussels sprouts
White Burgundy

**Grilled Chicken Breasts with Apricot, Raisin, and Marsala Sauce**
Sautéed green beans
Couscous with pistachio nuts
Sauvignon Blanc or hot mint tea

**Hickory-smoked Whole Chicken with Kansas City Barbecue Sauce**
Grilled sweet potatoes
Creamy coleslaw
Corn bread
Beer, iced tea, or lemonade

**Vine-smoked Chicken Breasts with Herbs and Mustard-Cream Sauce**
Grilled halved red potatoes
Grilled red onion wedges and
    grilled sliced zucchini with
    balsamic vinegar
Chardonnay

**Mesquite-smoked Chicken Breasts with Grilled Poblano-Tomatillo Sauce**
Black bean salad
*Chilaquiles*
Mexican beer or fresh limeade

**Smoked Sesame Chicken on a Bed of Bitter Greens**
Grilled fennel slices
Grilled beet slices
Green onion pancakes
Moselle or Riesling

# GRILL BOOK
*List of Menus*

**Butterflied Leg of Lamb with
    Zinfandel Sauce**
Grilled Turnips
Braised Spinach with Toasted Almonds
Crusty Italian Bread

**Veal Chops with Gruyère
    and Prosciutto**
Grilled Polenta with Pesto
Grilled Pattypan Squash
Roasted Red Pepper Salad

**Skewered Scallops, Zucchini, and
    Artichoke Hearts with Salsa**
Herbed Rice
Cold Lemon Asparagus

**Grilled Whole Trout**
Grilled Mixed Vegetables with Aïoli
Arugula, Limestone, and Red Leaf
    Lettuce Salad with Avocado

**Grilled Steak with Fresh Herbs**
Grilled Sweet Corn
Caesar Salad
Sourdough Bread

**Salmon Steaks with Chive Butter**
Grilled Japanese Eggplant
Grilled Scallions
Cold Pasta Salad

**Tofu Marinated in Sesame Oil and
    Rice Vinegar with Scallions**
Grilled Whole Chilies
Sliced Fresh Fruit
Cold Soba Noodles

**Rock Cornish Game Hens in
    Raspberry Vinegar Marinade**
Grilled Pears
Grilled Mushrooms
Steamed Fresh Green Beans with
    Water Chestnuts

**Sesame Flank Steak**
Grilled Whole Potatoes
Sautéed Fresh Okra
Sliced Tomatoes with
    Olive Oil and Basil

**Boneless Pork Loin in
    Sherry Vinegar, Port, and
    Prune Marinade**
Grilled Carrots
Herbed Potatoes
Tossed Greens

**Grilled Split Lobster Tail**
Roasted Garlic Heads
Butter Lettuce and Watercress Salad
Baguette

**Mixed Sausage Grill**
Grilled Red Onion Quarters
Red Cabbage with Apples
Dark German Bread

**Chicken Breasts in Many Mustards**
Grilled Gravenstein Apple Slices
Grilled Baby Leeks
Radicchio Salad

**Nam Prik Shrimp**
Grilled Zucchini
Tomato Pasta with Olive Oil
    and Lemon Zest

**Grilled Breast of Duck
    in Red Wine Marinade**
Grilled Crookneck Squash
Wild Rice with Green Onions
    and Mushrooms
Belgian Endive Salad with
    Toasted Pine Nuts

**Peanut Chicken on Skewers**
Rice with Lemon Grass and Coconut
Carrot Salad with Green Papaya

**Barbecued Baby Back Pork Ribs
    in Honey, Tamari,
    and Orange Marinade**
Grilled Yam Slices
Waldorf Salad
Corn Muffins with Green Chilies

**Grill Appetizer Party**
Topinka
Grilled Oysters and Clams on the Shell

# THE ART OF GRILLING
*List of Menus*

**Grilled Italian Appetizers**
Smoked Parmigiano with Assorted
    Breads
Bruschetta with Grilled Eggplant
Scallops Grilled with Basil and
    Prosciutto
Imported olives
Grape and fig bowl
Dry Italian white wine

**Tandoori Chicken**
Papadums
Grilled Broccoli with Yogurt-Cumin
    Sauce
Basmati Rice Pilaf with Mustard and
    Fennel Seeds
Raita and Chutneys
Lager

**Rack of Lamb with Port, Rosemary,
and Garlic Marinade**
Grilled New Potatoes
Sautéed Sugar Snap Peas
Tender Greens Salad

**Soft-Shell Crab with Hazelnut
    Butter**
Grilled Skewered Leeks and Mushrooms
Ribboned Carrot Salad
Fumé Blanc

**Burgers and Red Onion Slices**
Salad of Grilled Potato and Fennel
Sliced Beefsteak Tomatoes
Poppyseed Kaiser Rolls
Red wine

**Boneless Quail with Corn Bread and
    Escarole Stuffing**
Grilled Parsnips
Steamed Asparagus
White Wine

**Peppers Stuffed with Eggplant**
Grilled Skewered Summer Squash with
    Rosemary Oil
Sliced Fruit with Yogurt-Mint Dressing
White Wine

**Prawns with Spicy Remoulade**
Steamed Greens
Grilled Cornmeal Mush Slices
Chardonnay

**Tenderloin of Beef with
    Mustard-Mint Sauce**
Couscous with Sautéed Figs
Steamed Artichokes with Creamy
    Vinaigrette
Pinot Noir

**Calves' Liver with Sage Butter
    and Pancetta**
Tuscan White Beans with Grilled Red
    Onion
Romaine Lettuce Salad with Creamy
    Parmesan Dressing
Saltless Italian bread
Pinot Noir

**Lime-marinated Rock Cornish
    Game Hens**
Baked Black Beans, Corn, and Green
    Chilies
Mixed Green Salad with Orange
    Vinaigrette
Warm tortillas
Beer

**Ham Steak with Apple
    Cream Sauce**
Grilled Sweet Potatoes
Braised Escarole
Popovers
Rosé

**Grapevine-smoked Salmon, Trout,
    and Oysters**
Fresh and Dried Bean Salad with Chive
    Vinaigrette
Oven-roasted Asparagus
Assorted breads and herbed cream
    cheese
White wine

**Veal Roast with Marsala and
   Dried Apricots**
Pasta with Grilled Mushrooms
Radicchio with Walnut Vinaigrette
Bread Sticks
Red wine

**Hickory-grilled Pork Chops
   with Fresh Peaches**
Spicy Black-eyed Peas
Steamed Swiss Chard with Mustard
   Vinaigrette
Corn Sticks
White wine

**Rabbit with Pecan Butter and Apples**
Steamed Brussels Sprouts
Gougère
White wine

**Monkfish with Caper Vinaigrette**
Grilled Belgian Endive
Steamed Carrots with Cream
French bread
White wine

**Steak Teriyaki Rice Bowl**
Grilled Japanese Eggplant
Spinach-Sesame Salad
Japanese beer

**Thai Barbecued Chicken**
Snow Peas with Toasted Sesame
   Dressing
Silver Noodles with Cucumber, Carrot,
   and Rice Vinegar
Lager

**Spiedini with Balsamic Marinade**
Grilled Fennel
Pasta with Brandy-Basil Cream Sauce
Arugula and Red Leaf Lettuce Salad
Italian red wine

**Swordfish with Pico de Gallo**
Grilled Green Tomatoes
Corn on the Cob
Hard sourdough rolls
Beer

**Turkey Breast Smoked with Cherry
   Wood**
Three-pepper relish and cranberry
   chutney
Hearty Vegetable Salad with Herbed
   Aïoli
Custard Corn Bread

**Sea Bass on Bok Choy with
   Ginger-Garlic Butter**
Peanut-Sesame Noodles
Steamed Chinese Long Beans
White wine

**Hickory-smoked Country-style Ribs
   with Barbecue Sauce**
Herbed Twice-baked Potatoes
Wilted Red Cabbage Salad
Beer

# INDEX

*This book was
composed in Bembo types by
On Line Typography,
San Francisco*

*It was printed
and bound by
Toppan Printing Co. Ltd.
Tokyo, Japan*

*Design and production by
Ingalls + Associates
San Francisco*